G000146590

201241438

OWAIN ARWEL HUGHES

OWAIN ARWEL HUGHES

My LIFE IN MUSIC

UNIVERSITY OF WALES PRESS
CARDIFF
2012

WEST SUSSEX LIBRARY SERVICE	
201241438	
Askews & Holts	30-Jul-2013
B HUG	

© Owain Arwel Hughes, 2012

All rights reserved. No part of this book may be reproduced in any material form (including photocopying or storing it in any medium by electronic means and whether or not transiently or incidentally to some other use of this publication) without the written permission of the copyright owner. Applications for the copyright owner's written permission to reproduce any part of this publication should be addressed to The University of Wales Press, 10 Columbus Walk, Brigantine Place, Cardiff CF10 4UP.

www.uwp.co.uk

British Library CIP Data
A catalogue record for this book is available from the British Library

ISBN   978-0-7083-2530-8
e-ISBN   978-0-7083-2531-5

The right of Owain Arwel Hughes to be identified as author of this work has been asserted in accordance with sections 77 and 79 of the Copyright, Designs and Patents Act 1988.

The publisher acknowledges the financial support of the Welsh Books Council.

Designed and typeset by Chris Bell, cbdesign
Printed by CPI Group (UK) Ltd, Croydon, CR0 4YY

for Jean
who has shared my life in music

ONTENTS

I first met Owain at Caernarfon Castle in July 1979, when he conducted a concert to celebrate the tenth anniversary of my Investiture. Since then, his ebullient presence on the conductor's rostrum has become a familiar feature of many memorable events both in the Principality and elsewhere. Owain's sure touch with large musical forces means that his concerts are often huge affairs – never more so than when he kindly conducted the Philharmonia Orchestra, a vast Children's Choir and sixty harps at my sixtieth birthday party a few years ago!

His contribution to music in this country has been a very significant one, as the thousands of faithful fans of his Welsh Proms will testify. Less well known is his indefatigable charity work, his dedication to developing new music and his championing of underappreciated twentieth century composers such as his own father, Arwel Hughes. In the year of his seventieth birthday, I am delighted to salute him with admiration and gratitude and wish him many more years of happy music-making. His autobiography should make fascinating reading…

ACKNOWLEDGEMENTS

To my daughter, Lisa, for deciphering and typing my handwritten script. To Jean, Lisa and Geraint for their love, friendship and support. To David Hughes, leader writer with the *Daily Telegraph*, for his encouragement and guidance throughout. To Patrick Janson-Smith of HarperCollins for his direction through the preparatory stages. And to Clive Smart, former general manager, Halle Orchestra, and his assistant, Stuart Robinson.

LIST OF ILLUSTRATIONS

17. With HRH The Queen Mother at the opening of St David's Hall, Cardiff, in 1983.

18. Rehearsing for the Welsh Proms with Max Boyce, Nerys Hughes, Neil Kinnock and Cliff Morgan, in 1987.

19. With Jean, Lisa and Geraint, after receiving a University of Wales doctorate at Bangor University, in 1991.

20. Conducting Shirley Bassey at Cardiff Arms Park with the Royal Philharmonic Orchestra and a male choir of 10,000, in 1994.

21. With Jean supporting my leg in plaster, following the Pavarotti incident, in 1996.

22. Receiving the OBE from Her Majesty The Queen at Buckingham Palace, in 2004.

23. Owain Arwel Hughes OBE.

24. With Jean at the unveiling on Shrewsbury station platform in 2004 of a plaque commemorating the composing of 'Tydi a Roddaist'.

25. With Geraint, Jean and Lisa at Buckingham Palace, after being awarded the CBE, in 2010.

26. With Jean and our granddaughters, Clementine and Elektra, in 2012.

PROLOGUE

*I*T WAS THE AFTERNOON OF SEPTEMBER 11, 2001, forever to be known as 9/11, and I was in the final session of recording all Rachmaninov's symphonies with the Royal Scottish National Orchestra in Henry Wood Hall, a converted church in Glasgow. We'd put the final touches to the third symphony and I went to the room where the producer and sound engineer were sitting and we agreed that Rachmaninov's third and last symphony, was completed to our satisfaction. I was shocked to find that one of the orchestral players, who was not needed for the symphony but was waiting to play in the next piece, in hysterics, proclaiming that world war three had begun. We had one more piece by Rachmaninov to record, so I went back into the hall, and, without saying a word to the orchestra about the calamitous events unfolding in America, put down a take of Rachmaninov's beautiful orchestral version of his *Vocalise*. Then, during the break that followed, everyone became aware of the horrific devastation on the other side of the Atlantic.

I am in my element in the recording studio, but a break is always a welcome relief from the intense concentration and physical effort. I'm very lucky not to have suffered up till now from any of the back and limb problems that can afflict conductors. Unfortunately there was to be neither respite nor peace in this particular break. There was absolute chaos everywhere, with mobile phone messages and texts and groups huddled around portable radios and the one television set, everyone transfixed in total disbelief. Managers came to talk to us and there was a lot of discussion over whether the remainder of the session should be cancelled. We unanimously agreed to carry on. One of the first to speak up was an American sitting on the front desk of first violins. Finishing the session playing such a moody, evocative piece of music in such circumstances was quite surreal, creating an atmosphere I shall never, ever forget.

The scene at such a recording session can be quite revealing. We are in a converted church with warm, excellent acoustics. The sun is shining through the beautiful stained-glass windows that have thoughtfully and mercifully been retained. But, typical of an orchestra away from the concert platform and the watchful, public gaze, the variety of dress is extraordinary – some in T-shirts and jeans, some unshaven, some in shorts and sandals, anything that provides comfort in what can often be hot, testing conditions. This is a comfortable relief from the normal formal dress of a performance.

When we record in a venue away from a purpose-built recording studio like say Abbey Road of Beatles fame, a room for the producer and sound engineer has to be found some distance away, so that no external sound interferes with their listening. They wear headphones, or cans as they are known in the business, usually have a monitor showing the conductor and orchestra, a link to a phone to communicate with the conductor, and a red or green light to show that they are actually recording. A good relationship and mutual understanding between producer and conductor is essential, and I find that once a good sound balance has been achieved and agreed upon, there's no need to go back and forth during the session to listen to every take. If the producer or I want to do another take, there's usually a very good reason for it. I much prefer, and so do the players, to utilise the time recording. It certainly keeps up the momentum, and recording sessions are expensive enough as it is. When I first went to recordings as an observer in my student days, I used to be amazed at the time wasting as conductors and soloists disappeared into the sound booth, leaving the players reading newspapers or gambling in pretty serious card schools.

The journey back to London was a nightmare, with cancelled flights and no one having the vaguest idea what was happening, or what to do about it. I now found myself in a chaotic airport lounge, so, armed with a glass of real ale, I retreated into my own private world where I could reflect with some satisfaction on the completion of a major recording project, but at the same time, like the rest of the world, I was fearful of the future. With time to spare, I found myself contemplating life's absolute unpredictability, alongside memories of how often throughout my career I was faced with situations, often tragic, when a decision has been taken to carry on as normal.

I had been tipped off by some airline staff that there was one plane on its way that would definitely fly to London's Heathrow Airport. Already very late, we clambered aboard the aircraft, found our seats and settled down for the journey. Then we experienced that awful moment all air travellers dread when nothing happens, no movement, just silence for what seemed like ages. Things got worse. The Cabinet had met in London and obviously, not having a clue what was happening in the world, ordered us all off the plane. We were evacuated row by row. Every nook and cranny on the plane was thoroughly examined whilst we were individually, meticulously searched. This seemed to take forever but thankfully, in due course, we were allowed to re-board the plane and cleared for take-off, eventually landing at Heathrow in the early hours of the morning after a very silent, nervous flight, where my family – wife Jean, son Geraint, daughter Lisa and son-in-law James welcomed me home with obvious relief. Little did I know that in less than four years' time we were again going to face the agonising uncertainties, fear and horror created by a terrorist atrocity.

ORIGINS

I WAS BORN ON MARCH 21, 1942. World War Two was raging. My father, Arwel Hughes, was on the staff of the BBC in Cardiff and was being moved to different BBC regions to avoid the bombings. First Cardiff was hit, then Bristol, and so at this particular time he found himself in Bangor, North Wales. I was actually born in my father's sister's house, 6 Whitefield Street, Ton Pentre, in the Rhondda, the family later joining my father who was staying in Tregarth, a sleepy little village near Bangor. On my first birthday, my mother, father, sister Delun and I returned to 1 Colchester Avenue, Penylan, Cardiff, which was to be my happy home for the next twenty-one years.

Many people think I'm from my father's home, Rhosllanerchrugog, a village in north-east Wales four miles from Wrexham, because as a family we spent lazy, idyllic summer holidays there, and my Welsh as a result is peppered with its unique dialect and accent. I'm extremely fortunate to have spent so much time in Rhos, as it's affectionately and sensibly called. It meant I had the opportunity to get to know my father's family and share the experiences of a much older, totally different generation, particularly my grandfather William and my grandmother Katherine, known as Taid and Nain (North Wales Welsh for grandfather and grandmother), and Taid's brother Ewythr John. Both brothers were retired miners, and I spent many happy hours with them as they regaled me with gripping stories of their hard lives underground, both smoking clay pipes and shag, supposedly to relieve the effects of the coal dust. I can still clearly recall seeing the lines of buses taking the villagers to the mines in Hafod and Gresford.

The family home was named Arwelfa, a red brick house with a commanding view of five counties on a clear day. I've never been sure of the meaning of Arwelfa. It could be a place with a view, although my father always talked of it as a conspicuous place, the rear of the house visibly tall and prominent. One thing I'm sure of – the home is not called after my father. Far more likely, being the last of ten children, he was named after the house.

I used to love travelling from Cardiff to Rhos by train, as in those days my father didn't drive. The journey via Hereford and Shrewsbury was a real adventure for a boy absolutely mad on trains as I was, starry-eyed at the beauty, power and energy of those magnificent steam engines. Any excuse I could find, I'd be on Cardiff Central Station, trainspotting, and begging the driver to let me into his cab.

Taid, having worked in Hafod Colliery, went after retiring to Scranton, Pennsylvania in the USA to work as a miner for about five years. The first two children of Nain and Taid's marriage born in Rhos were Harriet Elin and William, affectionately called Uncle Willy. They both emigrated to America in the early 1920s, an ideal time to go to the States, as life was pretty hard in the UK. In their thirties, they settled in Scranton while Taid was still there, where Uncle Willy found work as a stonemason. He supplemented his earnings and indulged his love of music as conductor of the local church choir and a male choir called the St David Singers. The Americans loved to have an initial between the Christian name and surname, so Uncle Willy became known as William R. Hughes, the R standing for Rhos, the shortened form of his birthplace. He was, most unusually, a left-handed conductor, the first I'd ever seen, whose company, along with his wife Ceinwen, I enjoyed very much on his frequent visits back to Rhos. The sight of an enormous trunk carrying their luggage was always amusing as it appeared so grand in the simple confines of Arwelfa. On a recent trip with my family to New York, we visited Ellis Island, the former staging post for immigrants arriving in the USA. We all found it an emotional experience, imagining the anguish as some hopefuls were granted entry and others refused it, sometimes whole families harrowingly decimated. A number of trunks and suitcases had been placed in the entrance to the museum and bizzarely the large trunk right in the front was emblazoned with the name Hughes. Tales of my uncle's transatlantic journeys and the romantic names of American cars certainly added lustre to the fanciful imaginations of an impressionable young boy. They spoke of an apparently affluent life in America, but to Uncle Willy's credit his Welsh was fluent, still tinged with that unique Rhos accent. On his last visit to this country, he stayed for a week in our first house in Harrow, northwest London. Lisa, our daughter, had just had her first birthday on Christmas Day and Uncle Willy said to her in English with his American accent, 'I'll give you five dollars if you say *Willy*.' Naturally, Lisa said nothing of the sort, but then minutes after I'd left home to drive Uncle Willy to Heathrow to catch his flight, she clearly announced 'Willy'. On hearing the news in America, Uncle Willy promptly sent her five dollars.

My cousin Norma, eleven years older than I, was actually born in Scranton because her mother, Aunty Peg, one of my father's sisters, and her father, Ernest Howell, (Uncle Ern) had followed Uncle Willy's example and gone to America to seek a better life. Unfortunately, the late thirties was a bad time to find work in the States and with no prospect of finding employment they were forced to leave. Norma still lives in Chester, where I frequently saw her on my childhood visits to Rhos. I got to know her future husband Howard, whom I clearly remember resplendent in his Royal Navy uniform. He had served in the RAF during the war in the Air Rescue in Scotland, saving the lives of air crew shot down in the fierce battles. After the war, he couldn't settle down. He tried to join, of all things, the Palestine Police, but was deemed neither tall nor heavy enough. He eventually found a place in the Royal Navy as a ship's writer, dealing with correspondence and finance in such places as Hong Kong, Korea and Canada. He was on board HMS Belfast, a ship with a great history, now moored on the Thames between Tower Bridge and London Bridge.

Arwelfa was actually the home of Ewythr John, who lived there with his wife until she tragically died giving birth to their first child. Taid and Nain, who now had seven children, moved into Arwelfa to be with Ewythr John, and it was here that their remaining children were born – Aunty Peg, Ceri, who died at birth, and my father.

Danny, another brother, also worked in the mines, but left to become an insurance agent after contracting chest problems. He had two sons, Emyr Wyn and Gareth, whom I revered and looked up to as older cousins as they used to take me salmon and trout fishing at Bangor Is-y-Coed (Bangor-on-Dee), now well known for its racecourse. The only thing I remember catching was an eel! Emyr Wyn, the elder, followed his father into the insurance business. He sadly died some years ago, but I value and enjoy the friendship of his daughters, Rhian, Sian and Nerys whom I am in touch with, and visit, frequently. Gareth trained in 1952/53 with the West Kent Regiment and volunteered with the Army Medical Corps, serving on the front line when it was that evocative geographical landmark, the thirty-ninth parallel in Korea, the forgotten war. He afterwards studied at Cardiff Art School, embarking on a career as an art teacher. One of my earliest, sad, traumatic experiences was, as a schoolboy, having to find him at the college to inform him his father had died.

Over the years, I made many friends in Rhos. In fact my very first girl-friend, Stella, lived there. A crowd of us youngsters used to revel in the luxurious freedom of exploring the exquisite, peaceful countryside, the mountain walk to Llangollen and the inevitable soaking as we fell into the River Dee. Rhos mountain was also a favourite play area and had become legendary because in the war a German bomber, having missed Liverpool, dropped his bombs on the mountain before heading for home.

Another brother, fourteen years older than my father and known to us as Uncle John, was a real character. He had a car, and so was able to take us as a family around North Wales. Rhyl and Llandudno were always favourites – the miniature train around the lake in Rhyl and the dodgems on Llandudno pier – an absolute must. He changed his car frequently, in fact he made bartering and haggling with car salesmen a ritual challenge. It was always late at night and dark when we returned from these trips, often having stopped off at one of Uncle John's legion of friends. I always sat in the front between Uncle John and my father, seat belts not even thought of in those days, thoroughly enjoying the car's headlights cutting through the darkness and the bends of the tortuous North Wales roads. I attribute my lifelong love of driving to these journeys and I am sure they explain why I've always been a night owl.

Taid was a very kind, gentle, unassuming man. He had a sweet shop next to Arwelfa where he sold all kinds of confectionary and soft drinks, and he was idolised by all the children for his kindness and, more than likely, his over-generosity. I can still clearly recall the taste of Vimto and Dandelion and Burdock from his shop. Although small in stature, he appeared fit and strong, described by our doctor in Cardiff as having the constitution of a man twenty-five years younger, and despite debilitating and painful shingles in his forehead in later life, he lived until he was eighty-six. My Nain I remember as a large lady, completely opposite in stature from Taid. She must have been quite a remarkable, strong character, first of all to raise ten children and then to support and encourage them in their careers, especially my father and Uncle John. Like Taid she had, as a devout Welsh Baptist, an unshakeable faith, and she was highly respected in Rhos for her service in the community. She even laid out the dead ready for the undertaker.

I have strong memories of Penuel Welsh Baptist Chapel, of the reverence given to preachers and their sermons – Ewythr John could practically recite a forty-five-minute sermon word for word – and of the happy hours spent with so many friends in that carefree environment. It's quite peculiar how in a non-conformist chapel, families or individual members would always sit in the same seats, week after week, year after year. They were not reserved, but everyone seemed to be drawn to their own place by some instinct. Services started at ten in the morning, and we'd all walk together as a large family up the road from Arwelfa, past the Miners Institute, a popular gathering place for the colliers to relax in, which also housed a theatre. It was known locally and affectionately as the 'Stiwt', Rhos-short for institute, and I will forever remember its clock, which clanged very loudly every quarter of an hour. I'm delighted to say that as a result of lottery funding, the theatre has been splendidly renovated with a well-equipped stage and an excellent auditorium, a great incentive for presenting concerts, and staging plays and musicals. The clock still clangs.

Having arrived at Penuel Chapel, we were greeted from the seat behind us by a contemporary of my father's, Elfed Davies, his wife Heulwen and daughter Calan. Elfed became a Welsh Baptist Minister, becoming one of Wales's most brilliant preachers, his understanding of life's problems backed up by impressive theological and academic knowledge. By chance, Calan has become a close, long-standing friend of my family. She married a Liverpudlian, Malcolm McGreevy, whose work as chief executive of various hospitals meant that they spent some time in London, hence the friendship. Calan, I'm glad to say, still speaks Welsh with the unique, unmistakable accent and dialect of Rhos.

Cricket in the garden of Arwelfa was an absolute joy for me as I emulated the exploits of the stars of the 1953 Ashes win – Denis Compton's famous leg sweep down on one leg being a particular speciality. I remember that there was a corrugated-iron-sheeting cinema called the Pavilion next door, from which you could hear all the action, and my imagination ran riot as I first became aware of the power of music in films.

Some others think I'm from the Rhondda, although a few weeks as a baby in my aunt's house hardly qualifies me for residency. However, my birth is registered in Pontypridd alongside such famous names as Tom Jones, the champion boxers Tommy Farr and Howard Winstone, and singers Sir Geraint Evans and Stuart Burrows.

My father had two sisters living in the Rhondda, Lucy with her husband Tommy in Ton Pentre, in whose house I was born, and Sally with her husband Bryn, one mile up the valley in Treorchy. My sister, my brother Ieuan – the latest addition to the family – and I used to spend school half-term holidays with them, usually staying in Ton where Uncle Tommy had built the most amazing train collection. It filled two levels of an upstairs room and I would stand in the middle, completely surrounded by track and trains, as if it were my very own railway network. There were stations, level crossings, shunting yards, engines, passenger carriages, coal and goods trucks, all under my control. It was just sheer paradise.

In the late forties and early fifties, the religious and choral traditions of the Rhondda were still alive and thriving. Preachers were much respected, famed for their stirring sermons and rejoicing in such names as Jubilee Young. There was a wonderful story doing the rounds that Jubilee Young's nephew, on entering the ministry, decided to call himself Young Jubilee, hoping to benefit from the association with such a famous name. However, the Rhondda, well known for its wicked sense of humour, eventually nicknamed him *The Man from Uncle*, after the spoof spy TV series popular in the sixties.

I was too young to appreciate, let alone understand, these lengthy sermons, but exposure to the singing in the valleys was very much a part of my life. There were choirs everywhere, mixed, male and female, in village halls, chapels and wherever people gathered together. The male tradition was particularly strong and I had the good fortune to be on the doorstep of one of the most famous choirs, the Treorchy male. Its conductor at the time was the hugely charismatic John Haydn Davies. In many ways he was typical of the influential people of the period, locally educated and trained for the teaching profession. Musically literate, dedicated and enthusiastic, his effect on the choir was dramatic, and he was someone whom I came to admire greatly. However, the tradition I grew up in paled into insignificance compared with the shenanigans of the late nineteenth and early twentieth centuries. It's impossible to imagine now, but such was the rivalry between the choirs, especially in the tight-knit communities of the South Wales valleys, that after competitions, fighting used to break out in the streets.

The discovery of rich seams of the finest coal, known as black diamond or black gold, had transformed the social landscape. The population grew at a frightening pace, with whole communities packed together, creating a highly combustible atmosphere. Working conditions were immensely harsh, and, coupled with deprived living conditions and poor standards of health, especially among children, collective solace was found in singing. Male choirs proliferated so it was natural, after a hard day's work in the dreadful conditions underground, to congregate in the local pub at night. However, all the singers had fierce loyalty to their own villages and the tribal intensity at the local and national eisteddfodau – competitions – brought out the best and worst elements in their nature. This I suspect is where that peculiar form of Welsh jealousy – *cythraul canu* – the devil in song – took root. As time went by, the valleys saw a growth in large mixed choral societies, many attached, through the rise of nonconformity, to chapel choirs and often 300–500 strong. They regularly performed, sometimes with orchestra, the choral classics. In fact there were so many performances of oratorios and celebrity concerts that quite a number of professional singers, many based in London, not only gained vast experience but also forged lucrative and successful careers, travelling all over Wales.

Like Taid and Ewythr John before him, Uncle John also began his working life as a miner, but with real grit and determination he studied music at night after a hard day toiling down the pit. His endeavours resulted in a scholarship to the University of Wales, Aberystwyth, where he graduated with a B. Mus. He became organist and choirmaster of Noddfa Baptist in Treorchy, a huge chapel with a seating capacity of 1450, one of the largest in Wales. Just imagine what choral singing must have been like in those days when a nonconformist chapel could sustain the appointment of an organist and choirmaster, a situation that is still normal practice in the Church of England.

In 1928, my Uncle John trained and conducted the Eisteddfod choir when the National Eisteddfod was held in Treorchy. In one week they performed, with the London Symphony Orchestra, three choral masterpieces – Bach's *St Matthew Passion*, Mendelssohn's *Elijah* and Elgar's *Dream of Gerontius*, composed only twenty-eight years earlier. What an amazing feat, not only of true dedication to hours and hours of learning and rehearsing, but also the physical and musical stamina required for such a marathon of music-making. It brings into sharp focus the stark truth about the sad state of choral singing in Wales today, particularly the performances of oratorios and large-scale works. The mining industry, the catalyst for the breathtaking rise and success of the 'land of song' is now completely dead, while the chapels and churches in the valleys, once the bedrock of choral singing, hardly exist, the buildings either turned into Indian restaurants or clubs, knocked down altogether, or, saddest of all, left to rot and decay, a cruel reminder of the demise of Christian worship. Even Noddfa, Treorchy, where my Uncle John conducted such magnificent choral forces no longer exists, gone for ever.

I saw this at first hand when filming a series of programmes called *Codi Canu* for S4C, the Welsh language channel. It was a development from two previous series where choirs were created from scratch in rugby clubs, most of the participants having no previous experience of singing in choirs, with the aim of resurrecting singing on the terraces of Welsh rugby clubs. The intention of the new series was firstly to show in graphic detail the ghastly images of the crumbling chapels, the devastating legacy of the decline of industry, in particular mining, and the dire social effects on communities. This vision was to be offset with the creation of four large choirs, initially with what turned out to be an optimistic ceiling of 150 voices, in four Welsh valleys – Rhondda centred on Porth, the Swansea valley in Morriston, the Nantlle valley in Bethesda, and Rhosllanerchrugog. The choirs were to be formed solely for the television series, to show the exciting possibilities and extensive, high-class repertoire available to large mixed choirs.

Paradoxically, the attempt to create the choirs served only to highlight the depleted state of mixed choral singing in Wales. The four choir trainers did an admirable job, but were faced from the outset with a number of difficulties, not least, an underestimation of the task ahead. Initial numbers were poor, and despite a valiant effort, struggled to improve. There was confusion about whether singers could have previous choral experience, while local small choirs were afraid that the new choirs would usurp their importance. They were zealous in guarding their territory. Certainly, proof that *cythraul canu*, the devil in song, that peculiar form of Welsh jealousy that seems to afflict music, was still alive and kicking. The other serious problem was a lack of men. All the choirs suffered from this, the main reason being the stubborn refusal of most male choirs to support the venture, let alone participate in a concept involving mixed choirs. Rhos, surprisingly, with two large male choirs in one village, had only one male turn up for the first rehearsal, despite a healthy contingent of females, and it was only due to heartfelt imploring that a number of the Rhos Male Choir eventually joined, agreeing to rehearse the music for half an hour after their own rehearsal. The choir, with its rich, balanced sound, easily won the final competition, proving that by overcoming suspicion and egos and the curse of jealousy, it is possible to create a large mixed choir.

My own musical experience must have begun at a very early age, most likely way before I was aware of its influence. My father was a highly gifted keyboard player from a very young age, quite astonishing when one thinks of his upbringing as the tenth and youngest child of a mining family with no musical heritage whatsoever. He went to the Royal College of Music in London to study composition and organ, a courageous decision, not to say a huge financial burden considering his background. I'm reminded of my great friend and colleague, John Lill, who, with a similar humble upbringing in London's East End, now enjoys a highly successful career as one of the world's great concert pianists. I have always had the utmost admiration for my Taid and Nain, for their vision, strength of purpose and unshakeable belief in the development of that talent. My father studied composition under that musical giant Ralph Vaughan Williams, whose influence was profound not only as an inspiring teacher but also as a gentle, caring father figure in what must have been a very lonely existence in the sprawling metropolis.

The establishment of a new BBC Centre in Cardiff was a fortunate and timely occurrence for my father and he remained in the BBC fold until his retirement as Head of Music in 1971. My father joined BBC Wales in Cardiff in 1935, as a studio assistant, at the same time as Mansel Thomas, who began his twenty-nine year tenure at the BBC as music assistant and deputy conductor. Together, they brought a fresh impetus into Welsh music, both composers, London-educated, eager and ambitious. I was infatuated with the idea of broadcasting. My earliest memories of the BBC were the studios in 39 Park Place, entered into through a stone archway, which for a little boy must have appeared awfully grand. The BBC Welsh Orchestra established its base at Ebeneser Chapel School Room, in Charles Street, and any excuse I could find I would be there, not only listening to the orchestra, but fascinated with the ethos and magic of broadcasting. At home I used to hang microphones on strips of cord I had draped around the lounge, creating my own broadcasting studio and copying the sound assistants as they manipulated the equipment to get the best effects. But it was the red light that dominated everything. It's quite amazing that so simple a device can have such a dramatic effect, signalling a live broadcast and creating instant tension. To this day, a red light is like a surge of life blood, literally switching on intense concentration in me.

I have another childhood memory I can still clearly picture in my mind. Early one evening, during those enchanting, summer holidays in Rhosllanerchrugog, my brother, sister and I, together with my mother and father, went for a run in Uncle John's car. It was obvious that the three adults had a lot to talk about, and it was suggested that we three children would walk ahead to the River Dee, probably at Bangor Is-y-Coed, or Overton, and they would catch us up. It much later transpired that my father, who had already been a guest conductor of the BBC Welsh Orchestra, had been told he was to become its principal conductor. Whilst in Rhos that day, he had heard on the radio that Rae Jenkins, a popular showman from the wartime Tommy Handley comedy variety programme *ITMA* (It's That Man Again) had instead been appointed conductor of the orchestra. As time went on, my father was to become a household name on radio, conducting the orchestra as a guest in the orchestra's early classical repertoire. My father was also very involved in the region's early television output, conducting the popular Sunday lunchtime programme, *Croeso*. However the most enduring legacy of my father and Mansel Thomas's television output, was the hymn-singing programme, *Dechrau Canu, Dechrau Canmol*, conducted by Mansel, with my father at the organ, recorded in different chapels throughout Wales. As a result of this success, they were both instrumental in creating the nationwide English version, *Songs of Praise*. I sang in that first broadcast which took place in Tabernacl Chapel, Cardiff, which was spacious enough to accommodate a large congregation and graced with a really superb organ. The programme is still a national institution, having passed its golden jubilee.

It has been said, and I readily agree, that my father's resolute dedication to the improvement of musical standards in Wales had a detrimental effect on his own compositional development and output, and I certainly saw at first hand his unselfish support of his fellow composers Grace Williams and Daniel Jones, and his practical encouragement of the younger generation such as Alun Hoddinott and William Mathias. Thus it was in this environment that my life was to unfold. My father used to compose at night when his work at the BBC was done and so, when I was supposed to be asleep, I was fully aware of him playing his compositions on the piano. When, therefore, I finally heard his compositions publicly performed, I instinctively knew the music, having heard their ruminative creation into the early hours, either consciously or perhaps subconsciously, while asleep.

Music filled the house. My mother, Enid, played the piano and organ, my sister learnt the clarinet, my brother the bassoon, and I, the piano. Radio, or the wireless as it was then called, was constantly on, so I heard and loved from a very young age an extensive range of orchestral and choral music. Over the years, through this medium, I was able to feel part of momentous musical occasions. One such was the much anticipated and heralded first performance of Benjamin Britten's *War Requiem*, commissioned for the consecration of Coventry Cathedral after its destruction in the Second World War Blitz. Its impact on me, thanks to the immediacy of radio, was stunning and in later years it became a vital addition to my own choral repertoire. From a young age, the music of Sibelius had appealed to me, and one evening, I listened to a live broadcast of Sir Malcolm Sargent conducting the Finn's fifth symphony. The news at nine o'clock began with the announcement that Sibelius had just died, leading to a newspaper front-page heading the next morning – 'Sibelius dies as Sargent conducts his fifth symphony'. I avidly relished listening to the Henry Wood Promenade Concerts, my imagination soaring as I listened to such evocative names as Sir Malcolm Sargent and Basil Cameron. Little did I know then what fate had in store for me, destined to come under the influence of another of those illustrious conductors, Sir Adrian Boult.

The gramophone was certainly a wondrous way to reach music in one's own time and space. One day, I was at home recuperating from one of the usual childhood illnesses – measles or something – feeling much better, but not yet allowed back in school. Rummaging around in a cupboard, I found a vinyl record. I was instantly struck by this wonderful music, and on listening to both sides, saw it was the symphony No. 4 by Brahms. However I had inadvertently begun with the second side, so my first introduction to a work that was to become one of my favourites, and play an important part in my conducting career, was the Scherzo. It has been described as perhaps the greatest scherzo since Beethoven, and I must certainly have been gripped by its bursting energy, fizz and spring. I can also vividly recall first hearing Verdi's Requiem on scratchy old seventy-eight discs, with the orchestra and chorus of La Scala, Milan, conducted by Toscanini. I was completely bowled over by the helter-skelter, downward rushing of the strings and cataclysmic, thunderous power hurled out in the Dies Irae. I couldn't believe anyone could write such music.

two
SCHOOLDAYS

IT MIGHT COME AS QUITE A SURPRISE to many people who have known me over so many years as a conductor that my original intention was to enter the ministry as a Welsh Baptist Minister. So, having spent all this time explaining where I'm not from, I'd better reveal all, and admit proudly, that I'm a Cardiffian. Cardiff was a tough city when I was growing up. The Tiger Bay of Shirley Bassey fame still existed, with the railway line from London via Newport creating a definite barrier between central Cardiff and the docks. The local Cardiffians could be real characters, very much like the Cockneys in London, who have such a distinctive accent as well as their unique rhyming slang. Cardiff also has a very pronounced accent, not South Wales Welsh at all, but throaty and open, characterised by this typical rhyme – 'ark, ark the lark in Cardiff Arms Park'. This is topped by the ultimate Cardiff rhyming couplet – 'I'm Cardiff born and Cardiff bred and when I dies I'll be Cardiff dead.'

I began my school days in Marlborough Road Infants, starting earlier than the normal age of five because I was apparently pining after my sister, Delun, who was just a year older. The years in the junior school I remember as being very happy and carefree, with good teaching and discipline, but with plenty of encouragement and freedom to participate and perform in a variety of activities. Mrs Stewart taught us in our final year, the year of the eleven-plus exam, and I can see her now, sat on a high stool, encased by a wooden lectern, in the corner of the classroom by the window.

I was already keen on sport and even now I can clearly feel the tension building on a Friday morning, waiting nervously for Mr Thomas to emerge from the next-door class through the interconnecting door, usually in his trademark brown suit, with the list of boys chosen to play in the school football team the next morning. The school gave us navy blue shorts and we provided our own white shirts. I know it's a far cry from the splendid kit of today, but they were our school colours, and my, was I proud. We used to play on Roath Park, council-owned playing fields which were a short stroll down Penylan Hill where I lived. Our pitch was bordered behind one goal and one touchline by a stream. Inevitably, misplaced shots would land in the water, and it must have been hilarious for the bedraggled, forlorn, wet spectators watching us chasing footballs if the stream had become fast flowing in the winter. I loved these matches with the spiky rivalry between local schools, and the park was a happy, out-of-school playground for many of us.

I used to sleepwalk and one night my father caught me outside the house on the pavement. He asked me where I was going and apparently, still sleeping, I replied, 'I'm off to the park to play baseball,' the summer game in Cardiff. During those halcyon days, I made many friends, but my special pal was a girl called Diana Walsh, stunningly beautiful, with long, blonde hair. Tragically, years later, she was an air hostess on a British Eagle flight which came down on an *autobahn* in Germany.

The eleven-plus exams for entry to a high school now seem an age away, but they must have been anxious times for our parents. They were a defining moment in our lives but we pupils, I'm sure, were enveloped in that glorious, blissful innocence of childhood. Thankfully I passed, so I could nominate the school I wished to attend. I must have been a little awkward even at that age because I refused to go to the so-called posh school, Cardiff High, because it had school on Saturday mornings. Saturday morning was sancrosanct, reserved only for sport! I chose instead Howardian High School, formerly Howard Gardens, in the square of that name which was close to the centre of Cardiff. It was an all-boys school, as all high schools in Cardiff in those days were single sex.

It was September 1953, the year the newly named school opened its gates for the first time in its new location off Colchester Avenue, quite close, in fact walking distance from my house. There we were, proud, excited, nervous and anxious as we approached the brand new, red-brick building. Unfortunately, the road leading to the school hadn't been finished, so we had to fight our way through Saharan dust storms in our shining new school uniforms and, as the winter rains came, we sloshed through a sea of orange-brown mud. The playing fields hadn't been completed either, and for the first two years we played all our rugby and cricket matches on borrowed pitches. During those years, we must have traversed most of Cardiff in double-decker local transport buses to play inter-school as well as house matches.

One of the many tasks we were given in those early years was to clear the fields alongside the school of stones and any other rubbish and detritus, so that we could, in time, have our own sports pitches. Mounds and mounds of stones, like ancient burial sites, were the result of our labours, and although we must have grumbled endlessly at the ignominy of toiling away on our hands and knees, the resultant rugby, cricket and athletics facilities gave us all a real sense of pride, satisfaction and camaraderie. I was in Drake house – the others being Hawke, Rooke and Wolfe – our colours, light blue. I loved the cut and thrust of competition between the houses, not only in sport, but also in the academic arena, and especially at the Eisteddfod, which took place on the morning of 1 March, St David's Day. The school Eisteddfod followed the procedure of any Eisteddfod in Wales, a competition involving individual singers, instrumentalists and choirs as well as prose, poetry and recitation. The rivalry was fierce, and boys came up with all sorts of ideas just to get points. One day when I was in the upper sixth, my final year, my brother Ieuan came home to say that his partner in the recorder duet had been taken ill, so I was given a crash course in the intricacies of recorder-playing. On stage the next day, we were doing really well until we looked at each other, setting us both into fits of the giggles, much to the surprise of the adjudicator who I think thought it was part of the act. My form master scornfully accused me of turning the Eisteddfod, the pride of the school calendar, into a music hall! The afternoon, much to our delight and relief , was a half-day holiday. Funnily enough, an Old Howardian came to see me after a Royal Philharmonic Orchestra concert recently and reminded me of that hilarious event – after fifty-one years.

It is no exaggeration to say that my schooldays were very happy and productive, with every hour of the day filled to the brim with all kinds of activities. Like all schoolboys, we were quick to recognise the different qualities and characteristics of the masters, some good, some pretty nasty, but mostly they were much liked and respected. One of the real characters was the English master, Dewi Williams, who did the odd gig on BBC radio, so he tended to act his way through lessons, which meant that Shakespeare, Milton and Wordsworth became alive and fresh and there was nothing we wouldn't do for him. He organised groups of boys to speak at events such as Rotary lunches, dinners and debates, stimulating us to be creative. What an imaginative way to train and prepare us for whatever the future was to hold, and I believe he had a knack, an instinct, for recognising the potential of each individual. His real party piece was assuming the character of his alter ego, Squadron Leader D. L. French Williams, DFC, DSO and bar, a fighter pilot in the Second

World War. On trips away from school, he used to keep us spellbound with his heroics, blowing up ammunition trains, defending the country against bombing raids in the Battle of Britain or dog fights over France, and a wild account of parachuting into the channel and swimming back to shore in full uniform with his flying boots full of water.

Another character was Tommy Foster who is still talked of affectionately, even reverentially, by generations of old pupils. He taught Drama, French and Latin, his warning words to any misbehaving boy, while pretending to clutch their throats being, 'iugulo, iugulare – to strangle'. He led many activities, particularly the school plays, but his real speciality was cricket. In my first year, he collected a group of boys together every Saturday morning for cricket training, the precursor to today's squad training. He nurtured this group over the years until we became a superb outfit, winning the cup and league double. The semi-final and final of the cup were played on the Glamorgan County Cricket ground, which was then at the famous Arms Park, a dramatic, imposing, historic arena in the centre of Cardiff. What an experience for us youngsters to arrive at the Arms Park, not to spectate, but to play on the hallowed turf. The pavilion was the reverse side of the huge North Stand of the Cardiff and Wales rugby ground which towered over the outfield, and the pitch itself was magnificent and lush – a world away from those early, pitchless years at the new Howardian. Years later I understood the terror experienced by Tony Lewis, the Glamorgan and England cricketer as he described to me seeing the fast West Indies bowlers Wes Hall and Charlie Griffiths emerging, after their intimidating, lengthy run from under the shadows of the immense stand, to hurl their hard, red projectile at the hapless batsmen, helmet-less in those days.

However, the absolute, towering personality at the school was the headmaster, a Yorkshireman by the name of Archibald Sinclair. His impact and influence on the school was immense. He was resolute in his support of anything or anyone who would further the development and reputation of his school. His discipline was tight, yet we all knew that the needs of the boys were paramount, and that a first-class, all-round education, was essential. One thing above all else that any Old Howardian I meet anywhere in the world still remembers is the head's penchant for making a speech, especially during morning assembly. We loved his tirades, particularly if they went on long enough to miss first lesson, and especially if it happened to be maths. Whenever we alumni meet, stories abound about the head, with affection I must add. One such story I will always remember verbatim. There was a girl's school next door called Lady Margaret. Our head and the headmistress were obviously not on amicable terms, to put it mildly, so there was no communication between the two sets of pupils, the standard joke being there might as well have been a minefield in between the two schools. At one time it got so bad that we were forbidden to be seen with any of the girls, leading to the ludicrous situation that I couldn't walk to school with my own sister who was a year ahead of me at Lady Margaret. This subsequently led to these immortal, unforgettable words in a morning assembly, all spoken with a pronounced Yorkshire accent – 'It has come to my notice that some of you young thugs have been seen fraternising with those scarlet women next door. We must extirpate this moral gangrene, this cancer of the soul.' You really couldn't make it up. Extirpate is a word none of us would ever have come across but for our headmaster.

As I entered my fifth year in the school, at the age of fifteen, the head was to be the unwitting catalyst for a decision that was eventually to turn my world upside down and change my life for ever. The music master had left the school at the end of my second year, and as science was all important, he wasn't replaced. The Welsh master, Wynne Lloyd, a kind, gentle, caring man, kept the choir going, but at the end of my fourth year, left to join the education department of the BBC. So, in all innocence, I went to see the head, complaining that there was no music in the school, not even a choir. The head's words are indelibly etched in my memory. 'If you're so concerned son (Yorkshire accent) then do it yourself.' Looking back, I'm sure he meant, 'oh for goodness sake get out of here', a polite way of getting rid of me. As it happens, his thoughts went completely over my head. I took him literally and formed a choir of my own. In my first year at the school, my form room had been the music room and I remembered that there was a storeroom at the back. There I found copies of Mendelssohn's *Hymn of Praise*, taught the choir some of the choruses, and performed them in the Christmas concert. I know this might seem a little bit unusual, but I played rugby and cricket for the school, enjoyed drama and thought this was just another normal, extra-curricular activity. The love of music was obviously a very substantial element in my life, but for quite a while I had been responding to a calling, and it wasn't music.

three
CHAPEL, SPORT – AND MUSIC

ELSH WAS THE LANGUAGE OF THE HEARTH, and so with English spoken in school and Welsh at home as well as in Tabernacl Welsh Baptist, the chapel I attended from the time I could walk, I had the ideal, classical, bilingual upbringing. It's difficult perhaps for people today to imagine, let alone understand, the importance of the chapel in my life, especially one in the centre of a tough city, in an area called the Hayes. Today, the Hayes is bright and bustling, with St David's Hall, one of Europe's finest concert halls, at one end and huge shopping malls and a massive John Lewis at the other. In those days the area around Tabernacl was dark and dingy with dirty warehouses and broken-down, derelict buildings. There was a sleazy cinema across the road, the infamous Caroline Street – home of sex magazine shops and prostitutes – next door, and the prison just around the corner.

Childhood memories vary incredibly. Some are lost; others are imprinted indelibly on the mind, either for the inexpressible joy of recalling them, or for their unwelcome unpleasantness. One event every Tabernacl child always remembers and recounts is the morning service on the first Sunday of every month – the children's service. An important feature was that all the children had to recite, facing the congregation, a verse from the bible. This was delivered standing in the 'set fawr' – big seat, where the deacons sat. It was like a raised stage in front of the pulpit. Everyone's first effort was always the same – stuttering, jibbering and ending in tears. Then at last, the great moment when that first verse – everyone chose the same – was eventually, triumphantly delivered: 'Duw cariad yw' – God is love.

Looking back, the discipline of having to learn a different verse and deliver it before the staring eyes of the congregation, especially those of your own family, was the perfect training ground for anyone who was to have a future in public life. Performing in front of one's family has always been an intriguing situation, and many is the time wonderful orchestral principal players have confided in me their peculiar nerves when they have an important solo to perform, particularly when in their home town with their own family in the audience.

The minister of the chapel was the Reverend Myrddin Davies, a white-haired man, small of stature, but to us youngsters as we grew up, a giant. His care over us all was astonishing and there was nothing we wouldn't do in return. The chapel ran a youth club on a Friday night, and as we got older we were entrusted with being in charge of it ourselves. Many was the time in that dingy area of Cardiff that we had to deal tactfully with some dubious characters, or sometimes help prisoners just released from the prison. This was quite an amazing freedom given to us by Myrddin Davies, but he knew that by granting us this responsibility we would learn how to handle an assortment of sometimes difficult situations. It is no wonder that we all had such respect for him – a man with a sure knowledge and experience of human behaviour.

My home life I remember as being very happy and contented, immensely busy and productive, with every minute seemingly utilised to the full. I was in the very interesting position of being the middle child of three, my sister Delun older by fourteen months and my brother Ieuan, younger than I by nearly three years. We were very close friends and although different in character, enjoyed each other's company. The Reverend Myrddyn Davies, with his wise understanding from years in the nonconformist ministry, held a strong belief in the unique role of the middle child of three. He was of the opinion that finding oneself between an elder sibling who had naturally been fussed and worried over during the learning curve of bringing up a first child, and a younger one who enjoyed much more freedom, produced and developed a special character and personality. In my own experience, I enjoyed and relished what I perceived as my responsibility towards my sister and thrived upon my ever-burgeoning relationship with a brother who without doubt, even by his own admission, enjoyed far less parental restraint.

My brother and I were always kicking a football about and my sister and I would be singing whenever we had the opportunity. I actually had quite a nice boy-soprano voice but things went rapidly downhill when my voice broke. Eventually I was able to contribute to the bass section in mixed choirs, probably because I could read music well, rather than due to any vocal qualities. It certainly provided me with a thorough knowledge of the choral repertoire and, interestingly, the inner workings and intrigues of choirs.

As a family we were all very fond of sport. My father, being North Walian had been brought up following soccer, and so I was taken from a very young age to watch Cardiff City at Ninian Park. I particularly remember one Easter Monday derby match with arch rivals, Swansea. We had arrived late, probably because my father had been working, and found ourselves at the back of a very large crowd on the terraces. Being young and small, I was passed down over the heads of the supporters and placed over the wall. Can you in your wildest dreams imagine that happening today? I still follow Cardiff City, and went with my own son, Geraint, to the new Wembley Stadium to watch them play in their first FA Cup Final since 1927. Alas, we lost. However if I have a concert on a Saturday night I have to know, before going on the rostrum, the Cardiff result, as well as that of London Welsh in rugby, whom I have supported since I went to London as a student.

Cricket was a sport we all enjoyed watching and playing as a family. Wherever we found a suitable space, we pitched stumps, sometimes in the most unlikely locations. Perhaps the strangest outcome of one of our games was in the car park of Rest Bay, Porthcawl. My father prided himself on bowling leg breaks and my mother, who was batting, and trying to sweep the ball away, got her legs in a tangle and broke her tibia. The term leg break forever took on a new meaning!

My mother's parents, Dat and Mam to us, lived in One Melrose Avenue, the next road to ours. They both hailed from Carmarthenshire in west Wales, settling in Cardiff and becoming members of Ebeneser Welsh Congregational Chapel in the centre of the city. 'Penbont' was the name of their house and it's very strange but I have deep in the recesses of my memory the vaguest recollection during the war of hearing the air-raid warning and hiding under the stairway from the bombs. Although the recall is fuzzy, there must have been something in my sub-conscious, because years later, when I was about nine or ten the siren sounded – probably a test – when I was walking alone to school. I ran to the nearest house, absolutely terrified, and that memory is anything but vague, even now.

Mam was a tall, striking lady with long, white hair, very strict, but who cared enormously for us. Dat was a very kind, gentle, loving man with a round cherubic face, completely bald but with a white moustache. He ended his teaching career as a headmaster in Moorland Road, a tough district in the Splott area of Cardiff. His pride and joy was a Lanchester car with pre-selected gears using a lever alongside the steering wheel to choose the correct gear without using a clutch, a precursor I suppose, of today's automatic cars. As a family we often went on day outings together, particularly on Saturdays, to such places as the very popular, sandy, Barry Island, or probably my favourite haunt, the idyllic Southerndown, in the tranquil surroundings of the Vale of Glamorgan. Meanwhile Dat and I had become the closest of friends, with an easy, natural, almost uncanny rapport.

Delun, Ieuan and I, naturally, had an identical upbringing – the same local schooling, chapel three times on a Sunday, participation in chapel activities such as plays and concerts, and Welsh as our first language. I feel very fortunate to have had such an early, natural grounding in Welsh. Speaking English was never going to be a problem in bustling, cosmopolitan Cardiff, whereas there was very little Welsh spoken on the streets of the city, and none in the schools I attended. Eventually came the sea change which precipitated the dramatic growth of Welsh-speaking schools, gradually transforming the attitude towards, and the numbers speaking, our native tongue. My ability to switch easily between the two languages has been of immense benefit to me socially, and particularly in my career as a broadcaster, both on radio and television. My very first TV series as a conductor and presenter was the Welsh language music programme *Blodeugerdd*, which enjoyed much success with its variety of orchestral, choral and vocal repertoire. Its use of English subtitles, quite an innovation at the time, removed any language barrier and added greatly to the audience figures. This series gave me enormous experience in the dual role of conductor/presenter under the careful, loving guidance of the producer and director Hywel Williams, an absolute master of his craft and the doyen of BBC Wales TV at the time.

My first meeting with Hywel took place in a building owned by the General Accident Insurance Company in Cardiff. They were housed on the ground floor, and the BBC rented several floors above, nicknamed with typical BBC humour, 'Calamity House'. On arrival he politely took me to the canteen for coffee, and explained that he and his senior executives had seen me on television presenting a brass band competition. The final had taken place in Manchester, and the guest of honour who presented the winning prize was the Welsh heavyweight boxing legend, Tommy Farr, who had surprised the boxing world by only losing to the World Champion Joe Louis on a controversial points decision, when Joe Louis was expected to knock Farr out easily. I must have looked ridiculously tiny alongside this massive man, but we quickly warmed to each other, he being the gentlest of giants.

After a while Hywel began intimating that they were interested in my presenting and conducting a television series. The BBC in Wales was committed to broadcasting a certain number of hours a week in the Welsh language, opting out of the national programmes on the flagship BBC One channel. At lunchtime Hywel suggested we adjourn for a drink to the BBC Club, which was established in a large house along the road from the offices. I recall it being rather liquid, but after much talk and probably after I was well vetted and approved, the series was agreed upon. The recording day itself had to be meticulously planned, as the facilities were pretty basic. The studio was a converted church in the Broadway area, not far from the old Royal Infirmary. There was very little room for manoeuvre, with an orchestra, soloists and often a choir crammed into the meagre space. Very often Hywel's direction to a cameraman after taking a particular shot was to disappear behind a curtain to avoid being seen in another camera's shot.

We began the day of recording with a morning piano rehearsal in the studio, always useful, as it ironed out many problems, thus avoiding unnecessary time-wasting later in the day. The afternoon was a rehearsal session with orchestra, whatever vocal resources that were needed, and cameras. The recording was a rehearse-record session, recording in sections once everyone was ready, with breaks to rearrange cameras and scenery in the cramped space. Benny Litchfield, a local, very experienced freelance musician, arranged and prepared all the music. He also fixed the players on a freelance basis, as the series, although a music one for the BBC, by the BBC, did not come under the remit of the BBC music department. Our little band, excellent though it was, thus became disparagingly called, the 'Cowboy Orchestra'. It was quality exposure that was to be the catalyst for my own future TV career.

My sister, brother and I were brought up in the same musical atmosphere at home through our father's profession. However it's fascinating how much, or how little, that was to influence our individual developments, our career paths, and the whole structure of our future lives. In the high school, my sister and I tended more towards the Arts, whereas our brother favoured the Sciences. On leaving school, Delun decided on a career in teaching, and studied at Bangor Normal College, a teacher-training establishment stunningly located on the banks of the Menai Straits in North Wales. She specifically chose the Infants School reception class as her speciality, an area of teaching that requires infinite care, tolerance and endless patience, qualities which Delun had in abundance. Her love of music and her practical abilities would also have benefited her and the children.

Ieuan, quite early on, chose to be a doctor and enrolled in the National School of Medicine in Cardiff. This was quite a surprise as there was no medical pedigree in the family to influence him. He followed the medical route rather than surgery and specialised in paediatrics, becoming very well known as an expert in paediatric endocrinology. He is now professor of Paediatrics at Addenbrooke's Hospital in Cambridge. Ieuan also has a great love and knowledge of music which he puts down directly to his early influence at home. He regards music as his hobby and really enjoys his visits to concert halls and opera houses. On a visit to New York, he went to hear Leonard Bernstein perform Elgar's *Enigma Variations*, an interpretation that had caused quite a controversy when he performed it in London. Ieuan went to see Bernstein after the concert and asked for his autograph. When he just wrote a huge 'R', Ieuan naturally asked him what it was – 'Regal' replied Bernstein loftily, 'Regal', which puzzled Ieuan. To confuse him even further, I did point out to him that regal was an anagram of Elgar (as well as of lager, as one brass section dutifully pointed out to me on another occasion). Whether Bernstein was aware of this or referring to Elgar's music or his own performance, is highly debatable.

Ieuan was a medical registrar in the Accident and Emergency unit at University College Hospital, London on the night of 29 July, 1970, when a casualty was brought in unconscious after a heart attack. All the usual resuscitation processes were gone through but unfortunately to no avail. It turned out to be the world-renowned, legendary conductor of the famous Halle Orchestra, Sir John Barbirolli.

I undoubtedly must have been deeply enriched by the musical environment created by my father. His natural talent, particularly as a keyboard player and composer, was unmistakeable, and something to be admired and enjoyed. I must have unknowingly basked in this atmosphere, an influence however that at first appeared to lie latent. Although I had started conducting in school at the age of fifteen, I was already clear in my mind that my future lay in the Christian Ministry. I was very comfortable in the surroundings of Tabernacl chapel, the various services, the fellowship, and the reverent devotion of Myrddin Davies. In fact, for a school essay on the topic 'My Hero', I chose as my subject Myrddin Davies. My first attempt at a sermon was having to preach to him alone in his garden, with him seated comfortably in a deck chair in the warm sunshine and I, most likely, a mumbling, nervous wreck. I can still remember the subject of that maiden sermon – jealousy. Even though I was young, my all round, multifarious upbringing must have made me aware of the extreme diversity of human nature and behaviour. Perhaps I saw then that jealousy is the root of a great deal of evil, something I was to experience all too often in the future.

four
DECISION TIME

*I*T HAS OFTEN BEEN SAID THAT SCHOOL DAYS are the happiest days of your life. I had seven genuinely superb years in Howardian High School. Academically sound, sporting and culturally active, it provided me with a rock-solid foundation for the unknown trials and tribulations that undoubtedly lay ahead. Although encouraged by the school to further my education at Oxford University, I chose rather to study at Cardiff University, a constituent college of the University of Wales, with the specific intention of reading philosophy, before continuing my preparations for the ministry, studying divinity at the Welsh Baptist College.

Philosophy I found absorbing and thought provoking. It challenged me to analyse, reason and rationalise in a way quite new to me, a way of thinking that has influenced and characterised me ever since. A fellow student was W. J. (Bill) Edwards, a mature student already being prepared and destined to become a Welsh Congregational Minister. We spent countless hours listening to magnificent preachers, preparing our own services and sermons, and generally adjusting our minds to our chosen way of life.

Meanwhile, music-making was still important to me. I had formed the Cardiff Aelwyd Choir, attached to Urdd Gobaith Cymru – the Welsh League of Youth. This was an amazing organisation set up to encourage the youth of Wales to develop cultural and aesthetic skills through countrywide competition, performances, and a wide range of challenging outdoor activities. Generations of Welsh youngsters derived enormous pleasure and satisfaction from the support of the Urdd and I know with certainty that whichever path I chose the influence of the Urdd would have been everlasting.

I had also taken over conducting our chapel choir, Tabernacl, which under the superb guidance of my father had developed into quite a formidable choral outfit, progressing from a group barely able to tackle simple anthems into an ensemble able to perform the classical oratorios. Here again I was able, through first singing, and then conducting, to gain insightful knowledge of the choral repertoire.

The inter-college Eisteddfod was an integral part of University of Wales life. I had been mortified in my first few months to have been in the Cardiff University male choir that was booed off the stage at one in the morning in the Eisteddfod, held that year in Aberystwyth, because the boys were falling about drunk. I was asked to conduct the choir the following year and vowed I would never again be involved in such an embarrassing calamity. I managed to form a choir of ninety-six men with a quality of sound that turned out to be quite astonishing – huge rugby players with, surprisingly, the sweetest tenor tone, and sturdy, full-blooded basses, one of them being the red-haired Neil Kinnock. He still talks with immense pride of that stunning win, and how that time we were unanimously cheered off the stage. What made the occasion even more memorable for me was that the adjudicator was none other than John Haydn Davies, the conductor of the famous Treorchy male choir for whom I had such esteem.

It was now that I embarked on a period of agonising soul searching. It had become very clear to me that I had a gift for conducting. The actual physical process and movements were totally natural, as was the selection of tempi with their myriad complexities, and the rapport and communication with the performers. I have just read an article by a friend whom I greatly admire, the wonderful mezzo-soprano, Dame Janet Baker. She describes talent as God-given, something you're entrusted with, to be respected. This beautifully sums up the heartache I was suffering. Was I right to ignore a God-given talent? Was I sufficiently talented to become a professional conductor? I had spent years responding to what I honestly felt to be my future. My parents, naturally, with their strict, nonconformist upbringing, were extremely proud of my intention. Was I betraying their trust and belief in me, and that of others? Was I concerned that I would upset and disappoint them? Was I turning my back on a true, genuine calling? What mental turmoil. To this day I can clearly see my father sitting alone at the breakfast table reading the newspaper as I went to tell him my intention to pursue a career as a conductor. His response was typically honest and sage – 'I've been waiting for you to say so.' It became clear to me that I was the last to see what had become blatantly obvious to everyone, and

I admired his wisdom in discerning that the decision had to be mine, and mine alone. He knew better than anyone the cut-throat, capricious, insecure nature of the profession I was about to enter.

Such a radical change of direction meant a re-think of my educational needs, so I moved away from philosophy to concentrate on music, graduating with an honours degree. I had excellent lecturers in all the essential elements of music craft with the eminent composer Alun Hoddinott as my composition tutor. In future years I was to happily repay his investment by conducting many of his works. This extraordinary amalgam of the academic, the practical and the creative, provided me with a strong foundation that was to prove invaluable as I began my innocent foray into the unknown.

If I thought my deliberations as to my future had been difficult, they were as nothing compared with the traumatic tragedy unfolding in the life of the black-haired, blue-eyed girl whom I had befriended. Her name was Jean and she hailed from Pontycymer in the mining Garw Valley leading north from Bridgend, a market town midway between Cardiff and Swansea. Her father had died when she was ten as a result of years working in saturated, sodden pits. Her mother, Phyllis, was left alone to bring up Jean and her elder sister Margaret with a pitiful pension from the Coal Board – in truth, not a single penny.

I first met Jean as a result of that single-parent family trying to make ends meet. In order to obtain a singing scholarship to enable her to continue her education at Cardiff University, Jean had to undergo an assessment by her tutor who asked me if I could play the piano so he could be free to listen properly. So began our courtship, fortuitously, by our love of music and music-making. My first visit to the Proms in London, together with Jean, had quite an impact on me. First, the frantic dash up Exhibition Road from South Kensington Tube Station not to be late for the start of the concert, and then the breathtaking view of the colossal inside of the Royal Albert Hall from on high, behind the orchestra, facing the conductor of course. It was Sir Malcolm Sargent, totally resplendent in his tails and trademark white carnation. He strode in, bowed to the audience, and then dramatically turning to the orchestra, with no nonsense, tore into the crackling opening of Mendelssohn's *Italian Symphony*. It was the stuff of dreams.

Jean, at the time, had an uncle and aunt, Trevor and Nancy, living in Clapham Junction, South London, and so we were able to enjoy the enormous benefits that London, a truly international metropolis, had to offer. In addition to its vast historical and cultural heritage, we both enjoyed the sport on offer, with many happy hours spent at the international cricket Tests at Lord's and the Oval. Trevor and Nancy had a daughter, Elizabeth, who being an only girl, spent a great deal of school-holiday time with Jean in Pontycymer. On one such visit, she met John Lloyd, a superb rugby forward, a loose head prop (No. 3), and a loyal servant and captain of Bridgend Rugby Club. Rugby supporters, and players, are well known for their enjoyment of beer after matches, chewing the cud, and generally pontificating on the match just finished. Bridgend's home ground was therefore most appropriately called Brewery Field, after the Courage brewery next door. Jean and John, living close by each other, had attended the same schools since childhood, and through this connection, John and I had become close friends. I used to join him sometimes when he was out training. Although he had a growing reputation as a mobile prop forward, he was still at least five stone heavier than I, and he would finish our sessions together running around the field, with me on his shoulders, like a sack of potatoes. Nobody was more proud than I when he won his first international cap for Wales. It was against England at Twickenham. The Welsh National Anthem has a unique ability to conjure up different emotions wherever and whenever it is played. Watching John standing there in the line up, proud, but naturally nervous, as the stirring sounds reverberated around the vast terraces and stands of the home of rugby, was most moving. Wales won 11–6. An unchanged side was announced immediately for the next game, and thus began John Lloyd's illustrious international rugby career, becoming eventually captain and then coach.

One particular visit to London perhaps encapsulates my determination and resolve even as a student in those innocent days. Karajan was performing in London with the Vienna Philharmonic Orchestra at the Royal Festival Hall. I spent all day tramping my way around London to find a way of getting to the rehearsal the next day. I eventually found the concert agent and was given a pass. I was up at the crack of dawn and excitedly made my way to the Festival Hall on the South Bank. Imagine my crushing disappointment when, still proudly brandishing my pass, I was refused entry because Karajan, the day before, had thrown a tantrum and banished everyone from the rehearsal. I was absolutely furious and, probably spitting venom, I announced angrily and fiercely to the inky, black waters of the Thames: 'To hell with Karajan, I'll conduct there myself one day.'

Some time later, one Monday morning at the university, I knew something really bad had happened when I saw Jean, having spent a weekend at home, appearing with a tortured, haunted look of despair, and the red eyes and puffed face of prolonged crying. Margaret, her sister, had been diagnosed with cancer and the prognosis was not good. She bravely continued teaching in Bristol until eventually she was forced to return home to Pontycymer to be nursed in her last year by her mother. It coincided with Jean's post-graduate teacher-training year and my final degree exams. Jean spent every weekend at home helping her mother in what had become full-time care, and I would join them on the Saturday to do the heavy tasks of cutting wood, collecting coal for the coming week and any general fetching and carrying up and down the steep hills of the mountainside. Margaret was an intelligent, well-educated individual with a determined, independent streak, and insisted that she and I had a private hour, no one allowed to interrupt. We both valued highly those precious moments, a huge privilege for me to share confidences never ever to be revealed.

On Monday, 1 June 1964, I began my degree exams, sitting the final one the following Monday. Exactly a week later I graduated and Jean and I became engaged, very romantically, on the steps of my family home in Cardiff. There was no time, nor inclination for any further sentiment; far more critical responsibilities beckoned us as Margaret's life was now inexorably fading away. She greeted the news of our engagement with sheer delight and I was dispatched to the local pub to get some bottles of Mackeson Stout as she said this would be good for her. I had never been inside a pub in my life, let alone one in an inquisitive Welsh village. I blush even to this day when I recall furtively purchasing the 'demon booze' through a hatch in the side entrance. It was all so surreal, but on reflection, the perfect panacea. Jean and I stayed throughout with Margaret, grabbing sleep whenever we could, until she passed away, peacefully, in the early hours of Monday 22 June, aged twenty-seven. Truly tragic. Ever since I had known Margaret, despite her being seven years older than Jean we had always had an easy, friendly relationship. Throughout that final year when she was mostly bedridden and suffering greatly, we had cultivated, much to the joy and solace of Jean and her mother, something very special, private and personal. Jean and I are absolutely convinced that she tenaciously hung on to life until she knew that I was committed to looking after her little sister.

Meanwhile, I had been granted a place at the Royal College of Music in London to study conducting. My mentor was Sir Adrian Boult who used the college's third orchestra to let us loose and gain experience. His fellow conducting tutor was Harvey Phillips, a former cellist in the London Symphony Orchestra, whose knowledge and understanding of the workings of a professional orchestra and the technical and practical demands required to direct them, I found invaluable. Sir Adrian, to my enormous benefit, unlocked a completely new world for me. He had a direct line back to Brahms through his own mentor, Nikisch, and his profound understanding and interpretations of the music of Elgar and Vaughan Williams were cultivated through their personal friendships, and the prestige and honour, not to say the responsibility, of being the first to give life to their creations. I humbly sat at the feet of this self-effacing, unassuming master, luxuriating in his intimate revelations and insight. This was way beyond mere technical time-beating. I am still fascinated though by the natural affinity we had – he the tall, elegant, aristocratic Englishman, and I, this wild, ebullient little Welshman. However he didn't suffer fools gladly and I soon got to recognise the signs of irritation and exasperation. Any musician seeking advice on how to pursue a conducting career would inevitably be faced with a list of impossible obstructions, a test of how serious and suitable they really were. Sometime after leaving college and actively pursuing a conducting career, I had a phone call from Sir Adrian inviting me to his home for a chat. I was dumbfounded when he began by thanking me for being the only person to support and keep faith in his assistant Harvey Phillips. Sir Adrian had been well aware, without showing any hint of it, how many students tried to ingratiate themselves with him, even hilariously trying to ape his conducting style – one I might add that was quite unique to him and practically impossible to imitate. I replied that I was the well-rewarded beneficiary of Harvey Phillips's practical musicianship. In later years I had the honour and privilege of fulfilling Sir Adrian's trust and confidence in me by sharing concerts with him in his mid-eighties. A lasting memento of our collaboration was his signed gift to me of a facsimile of the original score of Wagner's *Siegfried Idyll*. Perhaps another clue to our relationship was that my father's composition professor in the Royal College of Music had been Vaughan Williams, and that my own enthusiasm and fondness towards the music of that great composer, coupled with Sir Adrian's unique relationship with him, proved to be an intuitive magnet.

Having already graduated with a strong academic background I was able to plunge myself into practical music-making, either through conducting, playing trombone or percussion in various orchestras, or singing in the college choir. Involvement with the choir enabled me to further develop my choral knowledge, one memorable concert being a performance of Britten's stunning, dramatic *War Requiem* within a year or so of its first performance. Every four years the orchestral and choral forces of the four London colleges of music – Royal College, Academy, Guildhall and Trinity – would combine. I was fortunate that one of those events occurred during my college years, and it couldn't have been more spectacular – Mahler's eighth symphony, the 'Symphony of a Thousand', so called because ideally it needs a thousand performers to do the work justice. It was Sir Adrian who was at the helm one very cold, snowy, March day at the Royal Albert Hall. Little did I know then how often I would frequent the Albert Hall as a conductor, even having the privilege of performing that very same, awesome work. Another milestone was taking part in the college's contribution to the 900th anniversary of Westminster Abbey, the highlight being Sir Adrian's emotional, powerful rendition of Parry's *I Was Glad*, music which had previously been performed at the coronations of Edward VII, George V, George VI, and Elizabeth II, in the same magnificent setting.

As a result of all these activities, I came into contact and worked with many, many students. The Royal College had a superb tradition of nurturing composers – Vaughan Williams, Holst, Britten to name but a few – and this period was no exception. The problem was that if any composers wrote an orchestral work, the college curriculum didn't seem to allow for them to hear their music and therefore develop their compositional skills. As I knew so many players I formed an orchestra specifically to rehearse student compositions. This benefited us all – the composers learnt from their mistakes and practical misjudgements, and the players sight-read swiftly and accurately, while I myself worked clearly and precisely as in professional sessions. The end result was a concert of the best compositions before critics, broadcasting organisations and publishers. One of these composers was David Fanshawe with whom I later collaborated, eventually recording his now famous *African Sanctus*.

Royal College of Music tradition was not only confined to music. Practically the first thing we were told on arrival at the college was that a pub in a mews around the corner was known, from time immemorial, as the 'ninety-nine', as there were ninety-eight rooms in the college. Whilst I was there, Queen Elizabeth, the Queen Mother, opened an extension to the college. The rooms are numbered from 100. There is still no room ninety-nine in the Royal College. I was always hugely proud of my time at the Royal College of Music, with its impressive facade and unique location facing directly up the steps towards the rear of the vast, rotund, Royal Albert Hall. Every morning after walking into Kensington Gore from High Street Kensington tube station I would pass around the side of the Albert Hall coming face to face with the Royal College of Music, feeling I was going somewhere really special. The

Director was Sir Keith Falkner and in his opening address to us students he quoted the eminent English composer, Gustav Holst, who insisted that the Royal College of Music should be placed on the summit of the highest mountain so that only people who really desired to study at such an establishment would overcome the challenge and succeed.

One day, quietly sitting in the back of the college concert hall in the annual prize-giving, I learnt that I had won the Ricordi Conducting Prize. Ricordi was the Italian publishing house famous for promoting the music of Verdi and Puccini, those twin giants of the world of opera. I duly made my way up to the platform to receive my prize from none other than Sir Malcolm Sargent. Ricordi had offices in different capitals around the world, and London's was based in those days in Upper Regent Street. Imagine my surprise when I arrived there to find the managing director was a Welsh-speaking Welshman from Anglesey, Arthur Owen. It was fate once again playing a card, for unknown to me this unexpected meeting was to have an enormous influence on my future destiny.

My student life in London was not solely spent in pursuit of music. Through contacts in Tabernacl Chapel, I had obtained digs in Harrow, North West London, with the Reverend and Mrs R. E. Edwards, a retired couple who had spent their lives dedicated to the Welsh Congregational Ministry. On my first Sunday with them I was taken to a Welsh-speaking chapel in Harrow, the members parking their cars on Harrow on the Hill and approaching the chapel on foot, down a narrow path. This was my first acquaintance with 'The Hill', home to one of the most prestigious public schools in the world, boasting Sir Winston Churchill as probably its most famous alumnus. As a youngster brought up in a day state school in a tough city the very concept of boarding school was quite alien to me, as was the sight of hundreds of boys dressed in morning coats and boaters bestriding the Hill. Meanwhile, I very much enjoyed the comradeship and long-lasting friendships I made through attendance and worship at Harrow Welsh Chapel, and I look back on the support and guidance I was given in those apprehensive, early days in London as being fundamental to my ultimate survival and development.

Weekends in London could be extremely lonely and as an antidote to serious music-making and exposure to some really fine musicians I used to watch soccer. The local club was Wealdstone, whose ground was behind a large theatre doubling as a cinema, an ideal venue for concerts and performances by the local amateur-operatic society. Alas, neither the football ground nor the theatre exist anymore, demolished to make room for a Tesco supermarket and its car park. My free Saturday afternoons gave me the opportunity to relax and roam London in search of sport. I derived a lot of pleasure, as well as much amusement, standing on the terraces as a neutral, watching such iconic teams as Arsenal, Chelsea and Tottenham Hotspur. Their respective grounds, Highbury, Stamford Bridge and White Hart Lane, were quite awkward to get to, and the travelling involved, including lots of walking to eek out my finances, provided me with intimate knowledge of the complexities of London's geography. To this day, that familiarity has proved indispensable in my nomadic life as a London musician, with concert halls, rehearsal rooms and recording studios scattered the length and breadth of the capital's sprawling conurbation.

Pursuing these Saturday adventures is how I first came into contact with London Welsh rugby club. Their attractive home ground is at Old Deer Park, situated right next to the Pagoda at the Richmond end of the Royal Botanic Gardens at Kew, one of the world's finest and most famous scientific, conservation and landscape sites. The open spaces around the rugby club have provided the ideal environment for a family-friendly sporting venue. Generations and generations of children of club members have enjoyed the freedom at the end of matches to play happily and safely, usually mud-stained, trying to emulate the escapades of the players. The quality of the rugby itself was always a joy to behold, with London Welsh enjoying a deserved reputation for exciting, open play in those halcyon, amateur days. Their exploits became the stuff of legend as London Welsh provided seven of the historic British Lions Test Team that beat the New Zealand All Blacks in 1971, including the captain John Dawes, the indestructible medical doctor, J. P. R. Williams, and the fleet-footed, flying, side-stepping genius, Gerald Davies. After many years, London Welsh rugby is still my relaxation away from the pressures and hustle and bustle of my professional life, and many is the time having landed at nearby Heathrow Airport, I have quickly and easily switched off in the company of my family and friends in the congenial, cordial atmosphere of Old Deer Park.

After lunch on a Sunday, in my student days, I would find my way to Castle Street Welsh Baptist Chapel in Eastcastle Street, just off Oxford Circus. As youngsters in Tabernacl, Cardiff, we had forged a close relationship with Castle Street, enjoying cultural and friendly exchanges between the two chapels. The minister at the London chapel was a very famous preacher, Walter John, renowned as a wise minister who established a peaceful sanctuary of worship in what could be a most unfriendly city. His son Lyn, whom I had befriended on our earlier exchanges, proved to be the perfect, welcoming host, not only for myself but also for many other Welsh students, as well as those drawn to London to find work. The afternoon Sunday school class for this disparate collection of individuals was taken by Walter John's brother, George, a chemist by profession. He provided the perfect environment for discussion, argument and debate, which rapidly established a powerful bond between us, still unbroken even today. My close friend was Meirion Thomas, from West Wales, studying medicine at what was then Westminster Hospital, and a particular soulmate of ours was a music student at the Guildhall, Helen Williams. She, along with various other friends, shared rented accommodation in some dubious areas of north London, and many a time those dark winter nights would be illuminated with hilarious goings on in their company. Some of these residences were pretty basic and run down, and one night, as we were trying to dislodge a stuck window, Meirion, the medical student, managed to slam the offending pane down on to the fingers of my left hand, thus nearly ruining my career before it had even started. Happily, there's always a silver lining, as the doctor back in Harrow who treated me by punching two holes in my nails with a hot needle, in later years became my own family's trusted and dedicated general practitioner.

Despite this accident, Meirion and I maintained a firm friendship, and I rejoiced in his growing successful career. Surgery was his chosen path and he eventually achieved enormous status as one of the country's foremost cancer specialists. I have never ceased to be amazed at life's strange quirks of fate. My coincidental meeting with Meirion and our subsequent long-lasting friendship resulted in a life-saving situation. One year, on holiday in Mallorca, Jean found a lump in her breast. We arrived home on a Bank Holiday Monday and that evening I phoned Meirion, describing the symptoms. He advised me to bring Jean in early the next morning, adding that he had theatre on Wednesday. I took the resultant tests myself to be analysed in order to save time, and by the end of the afternoon, Meirion knew it was cancer. He duly operated the next morning. Nothing could have been quicker and his surgical skills ensured an optimistic outcome. The specialist oncologist co-operating with Meirion was none other than Bob Phillips, a former centre for London Welsh whom I had known since my student days. After more than twenty years, Jean is fit and well, thanks to superb medical care, the fortune of chance meetings, and a lot of prayer.

It was during my time at the college that I was to experience an uncanny, mysterious phenomenon connected with Dat, my grandfather in Cardiff. It was a Wednesday night, and after a successful college concert, I went back to my digs in Harrow for a sensible night's sleep, as next morning, I was conducting the third college orchestra. I woke up feeling very strange, very peculiar, with an urgent, unaccountable need to get to Cardiff. I rang my father who duly met me off the train from London, and on arrival at home found my grandfather lying still and quiet in bed. My mother bent over him and whispered in his ear – 'Mae Owain yma' – Owain's here. That afternoon so that my mother and father could have a little break I sat alone with Dat as his life quietly ebbed away before me. It was so peaceful. Why I had that compulsion to get back to Cardiff will always remain an enigma.

five
GETTING STARTED

I WAS IN MY LAST FEW WEEKS in the Royal College of Music when I got a frantic phone call from Jean. We were getting married in Tabernacl Chapel, and the treasurer, Wynne Williams, a gentle, good-natured man, was also the Registrar for weddings. Jean had gone to chapel one Sunday evening and Wynne Williams had asked her for the marriage certificate. She said she didn't have it, to which the reply was, 'well, I am sure Owain's got it'. For Jean, this was clanging alarm bell time. She knew full well I wouldn't have a clue about such mundane matters. The result was that I had to dash back to Cardiff to resolve the problem. We both went to the Register Office and were met by a frosty-looking woman, with that weary, glazed, time-worn look of someone who had seen and heard everything, and suspicion was her first instinct. Because of the lateness of acquiring a Marriage Certificate, we had to apply for a much more expensive special licence, usually the preserve of those having to marry quickly. The lady eyed Jean up and down, especially as Jean kept insisting that we had been planning the wedding for nine months. Common sense prevailed and, armed with the special licence, Jean informed Wynne Williams, to everyone's relief, that the wedding could go ahead. Uncle John in his wedding address summed it up beautifully – 'Treasure her Owain, she cost you more than usual.'

My last term at the Royal College of Music was a hectic one. Having won the Ricordi Conducting Prize in my first year and generally getting fully involved in a wide variety of musical activities, I had been offered a further year at the college, which I was delighted to accept. It meant I could consolidate all the practical work already achieved and gain further invaluable knowledge and experience through exposure to some really exceptional instrumentalists, singers and composers, many of whom would eventually grace orchestras and opera houses worldwide. In that final term I had the honour and privilege of being chosen by the students to conduct a concert given by a specially hand-picked orchestra. The programme I chose was Wagner's *Overture to the Mastersingers, Le Tombeau de Couperin*, a beautifully crafted Suite by the French composer, Ravel, and an unusual work by Vaughan Williams, his *Job, A Masque for Dancing*. The Royal College of Music has a superb concert hall, with excellent acoustics and an aura that I found created a distinctive atmosphere – that tantalising tension of nervous anticipation. The concert hall has a balcony at the rear, and sitting in the middle of the front row was none other than Sir Adrian Boult. What a way to complete my student career.

Extra-curricular activities were not confined solely to sport and chapel. During my school and university days in Cardiff, I had derived much pleasure from the theatrical and light entertainment productions of a group known as the London Welsh. Prominent among them was a brilliant comic genius, Ryan Davies, who, like so many Welsh people, had sought work as a teacher in London. The joke going the rounds was that the education system in London would have collapsed without the Welsh. Many a truth spoken in jest, I wonder. Ryan, on turning professional, became a national treasure. His spontaneous humour, coupled with real, natural talent, enabled him to forge a very successful career, particularly in television. He died, tragically young, in New York, from an asthma attack.

I located the London Welsh Association in Gray's Inn Road, midway between Kings Cross and Chancery Lane stations. It was a Monday night, and I was responding to a call to join the London Welsh Youth Choir. To this day, I don't know where the 'youth' part came from as I was probably the youngest, and I was in my early twenties. I revelled in the friendship of professionals outside my sphere, teachers of course, a hospital sister, a science lecturer in Kings College, bankers, lawyers, accountants, you name it, they were there. The London Welsh Male Choir rehearsed on the same night and most evenings were rounded off with everyone joining forces for a resounding sing song, usually in the Calthorpe Arms opposite, as in those days the London Welsh Club was unlicensed. I should also point out that these were the days of alcohol-free Sundays in Wales, the law being that on a Sunday Wales was 'dry'.

Between the two choirs, I came into contact with a startling array of characters. Anyone thinking they were important, or behaving above their station, was quickly put down. There were a number of men called Gwilym Jones, and one of them became universally known as 'Gwilym Good-looking', because he prided himself on his sartorial elegance. Nicknames abounded – 'Dai Carpets' because he sold carpets in a London store, 'Dai Biscuits', as he was a salesman for a biscuit firm, 'Cliff and Dai Boxes', father and son undertakers, and my favourite, 'Dai Picasso', because he began every sentence with 'now let me put you in the picture'.

In the 1920s, dairy farmers in West Wales, particularly in Cardiganshire, sold their smallholdings and came to London because times were grim financially in Wales. They borrowed money from large wholesale dairies who at the time encouraged enterprise – so the Welsh farmers could run their own small dairies. In the 1960s, these large firms stopped lending money, so the individual dairies had to sell up. Many then bought properties and established Bed and Breakfasts, mainly in the Paddington area. This fortunately coincided with the tourist boom, particularly from America. They also advertised in Wales, and their proximity to Paddington station, the mainline terminus from Wales, ensured a healthy, successful business venture. The added bonus was that the hoteliers spoke Welsh, which guaranteed their visitors a warm, personal welcome.

I am forever grateful for having the opportunity to savour and appreciate the balance between my strict classical-musical training in the sometimes insular environment of a conservatoire, and my exposure to the real, outside world – to quote the haunting, first act aria in Puccini's opera *Tosca* – *Recondita Armonia*, 'Strange Harmony of Contrasts'. This dichotomy has proved to be not only enriching but has provided an essential equilibrium in my life – on the one hand to be severely single-minded, resolute, and professional in one's work, and on the other to have the ability to relax completely with friends, and most especially, the family.

So my student days came to an end and although I had had much pleasure, fulfilment and satisfaction, it was now time to move on. Jean, during these last two years, had been teaching History in Bargoed Grammar School in the Rhymney Valley, travelling by train every morning from Cardiff where she had rented a flat. Meanwhile, her mother, after the devastating loss of Margaret, felt she no longer wanted to live in Pontycymer, understandably, with such painful memories, and so she moved to Cardiff to live with Jean. Mercifully, there was a great deal to occupy their minds, as Jean and I had set a date for our wedding, 23 July 1966, which coincided with the end of my time at the Royal College of Music.

The wedding took place in Tabernacl Chapel at eleven o'clock on a warm, sunny, Saturday morning. The dress was formal, morning tails. My brother was best man, and the ushers were John Lloyd, and a long-standing friend from Urdd Gobaith Cymru days, Peter John. We had first met at the Urdd summer camp at Glanllyn, on the shores of Bala Lake in Meirionethshire, North Wales. We thought nothing in those days of swimming in the freezing cold waters, and it was at these camps I had my first opportunity to climb the mountains of Snowdon and Cader Idris. The evenings were spent in cultural activities, for there was a great deal of talent on display, the motto of the Urdd – 'to be faithful to Wales, my fellow man, and Christ', very much our guide and inspiration. Peter owned and ran a garage with his father in the Pembrokeshire village of Crymych in the gentle Preseli Hills. He was steeped in the Welsh-speaking traditions of that area – the chapel naturally, and creating and promoting their own entertainment. Drama was his speciality and being a fine actor, he used to regale us with dramatic monologues, his eyes flashing, and his celebrated red beard bristling. I was thus well protected and supported on my wedding day with a Welsh international prop forward on one side, and a large, muscular, garage mechanic, on the other.

The officiating minister, to our joy and delight, was of course the Reverend Myrddin Davies. He graciously allowed the lesson to be read by W. J. Edwards, my university colleague, now a Reverend himself, who was embarking on his first ministry at the Welsh Congregational Chapel in Llanuwchllyn, on the western shores of Bala Lake. The service itself was bilingual, and directed with gentle tenderness, understanding and benevolence by Myrddin Davies, fully sensitive to the mixed emotions being experienced by Jean and her mother. The singing in the packed chapel was truly amazing, the four-part harmony lending such richness and sonority that at one point Jean grabbed hold of me, afraid I was about to turn and conduct the singing.

In the usual frenzied preparations for the wedding, we had been totally unaware that we were in the middle of the first-ever football World Cup in England. I had hired a car, as we had planned a week's honeymoon in Bournemouth. This sounds pretty unadventurous by the standards of today's honeymooners, but we were very contented and anyway we couldn't afford anything more exotic. The start of the journey was hardly auspicious, with a two-hour traffic jam trying to get through Gloucester – there being no M4, nor Severn Bridge. After an age of motoring we stopped in Marlborough, where beans on toast in a local café had never tasted so good. We must have looked pretty incongruous dressed as one did in those days in a formal 'going away' outfit, but thankfully, both of us were completely oblivious to our surroundings.

Bournemouth proved to be ideal for our honeymoon – beautiful beaches, charming countryside and a relaxed atmosphere. I even managed to watch a couple of World Cup matches on television, I think much to Jean's relief, so she could have a few hours of peace and quiet. We travelled home on world cup final day along completely deserted roads. There wasn't a soul to be seen; even an Automobile Association (AA) box we passed had been abandoned, with just the latest score chalked up on the door. We arrived in my parents' home in Cardiff just in time to see Germany equalise minutes before the final whistle. Then, in extra time, came Geoff Hurst's hat trick and the rest is history.

Jean had obtained a teaching appointment with the Inner London Education Authority, and started work in early September at Hammersmith County, a fifteen-hundred strong comprehensive school for girls, in an estate behind the Queens Park Rangers football ground in the White City area of west London. The contrast between her former school and this new post was stark. In Wales she taught in an environment where the pupils were respectful, hard working and determined to succeed. At Hammersmith County on her first day, she was greeted with verbal abuse, indiscipline and clashes between an array of different ethnic races and cultures. Thankfully the school was blessed with excellent staff, a percentage of them Welsh. The headmistress was a Scottish lady who had married an Indian engineer, most unusual for its time, so a no-nonsense Scot with personal experience of ethnic differences was a pretty formidable manager. Problems were quickly sorted out. In time, Jean built up a firm relationship with these diverse pupils, and reaped much pleasure, as, often against the odds, these girls succeeded in obtaining successful student places or worthwhile employment. These years were not without incident however, and one Friday afternoon, Morwen Jenkins, the deputy head, who originally hailed from the Rhondda in South Wales, was stabbed in the back by a girl who that morning had been suspended from the school. The pupil later went to the local police station where she bragged of having just killed a teacher. Thankfully for Morwen, Hammersmith Hospital was close by so that a paramedic team arrived swiftly, and with great skill saved her life.

Jean and I set up home in a rented flat nearby. It was walking distance from the school at the top end of Wood Lane, just further on from the BBC Television Centre. I am sure my parents and Jean's mother were horrified at the tiny, sparse accommodation, but it was all we could afford, and at least we had our own place in which to live. Times though were tough. How on earth do you start a career as a conductor? You can carry an instrument around, even put a piccolo in your pocket, but where do you find an orchestra? I began to

pick up any odd job that would benefit my career – training amateur orchestras, choirs, even arranging and copying out orchestral parts for TV music
sessions so that I could spend time observing and appreciating at first hand the
precarious life of hard-bitten, tough, freelance professionals. Like them, I also
needed the money. At this point I unequivocally confess that without Jean's
teacher's salary, I would never have been able to pursue my desire to be a professional conductor. If I was to seek out contacts and pursuits relevant to developing a conducting career, I felt it was essential to have the space and freedom
to achieve this. Jean and I chose to accept this formidable challenge together.
She, with her hard, fatherless upbringing, was supremely practical, and with a
wariness honed by years of teaching, developed a natural, suspicious instinct
for reading people's characters. I was ever the enthusiastic optimist, but also
realistic enough to realise that, just as my brother had had no medical pedigree,
I had no pedigree for this precarious, freelance business. People thought that
because my father worked for the BBC, my path would be smooth. Nothing
could have been further from the truth as I found on entering a profession far
removed from the cloistered, protected world of BBC staff. Musically, I learnt
a great deal from my father, and his support and obvious delight in following
my career was something I shall always treasure. However our background was
still very much Welsh, with none of the great, centuries-old English musical
traditions, and certainly as a family we had no aristocratic financial legacy.

One of my first engagements coincided with the greatest tragedy to strike
Wales within living memory. For weeks the weather had been atrocious, and
on Friday morning, 21 October, 1966, I was stunned at the news of the dreadful, appalling disaster at Aberfan in South Wales. As a result of the endless,
unceasing rainfall, the giant coal slabs on the side of the valley had cascaded
down the mountainside and engulfed a school, burying 144 people, 116 of
them children. We all felt helpless being so far away, feeling the pitiful despera-
tion as television pictures showed the terrible suffering and grief. As it happened, the next day, I travelled to Wales, albeit to Conwy in the north. In a
strange way, it was almost cathartic, as I was able to share the collective sadness
of the nation, and take part in church services on the Sunday.

The actual engagement was to organise a week's choral course for singing devotees. I took with me as an assistant, David Fanshawe the composer,
who, like me, was embarking on an insecure, risky profession. He was a very
special character, quite eccentric in his good-natured way, and together we
encouraged this motley group of enthusiastic amateurs to give quite a decent
performance of Vaughan Williams's *Serenade to Music*. On that same Saturday

evening following the Aberfan tragedy, Jean was at home when she heard the most almighty commotion of police sirens. Soon afterwards, the TV *Nine O'Clock News* was full of the daring escape of George Blake, the infamous Russian spy, from Wormwood Scrubs prison, which to Jean's horror was only a few hundred yards away. Nothing was heard of him until he surfaced in Moscow, although we were led to believe that he had been holed up in a house around the corner from us for six months.

In the meantime I applied for, and obtained, a position on a conductor's attachment scheme organised by the BBC Northern Orchestra, now the BBC Philharmonic, in Manchester. It entailed spending a month with the orchestra and its principal conductor, and I was expected to conduct any work at his request, the orchestra's schedule having been given out in advance to give sufficient time to prepare the repertoire. It was an excellent idea and I relished and enjoyed the challenge. The first weekend was set aside to observe a guest conductor and to my delight it turned out to be Sir Adrian Boult. He had been engaged to record the oratorio *Job* by Hubert Parry, a composer Boult was later to champion vigorously. To his credit, His Royal Highness the Prince of Wales has now taken up the cause, and promotes the music of Parry with equal enthusiasm, backed up with considerable knowledge and understanding. Attendance at this recording had an added bonus, as I met for the first time, two singers with whom I would in the future have a splendid relationship both on and off the concert platform – the Welsh tenor Robert Tear, and the Cornish baritone, Benjamin Luxon.

I had been given accommodation in the home of the leader of the orchestra, Reginald Stead, who lived in the Cheshire village of Hale. We arrived at the BBC studio on the Monday morning and I was informed by the principal conductor, George Hurst, that he would conduct Tchaikovsky's sixth symphony, the *Pathétique*, while I was to undertake Haydn's Symphony No. 88. Alas, George Hurst spent all six hours rehearsing the Tchaikovsky, and to compound my frustration, the next morning he spent the first hour of a scheduled hour and a quarter rehearsal from 10 to 11.15 rehearsing, once again, the Tchaikovsky. He came to me and said he was sorry he had taken so much time, but as we had a live broadcast at 11.30 he would do the Haydn. Having sat on my backside all this time doing nothing, I replied that I was quite happy to conduct the Haydn. In the short time I was given, I topped and tailed each movement, rehearsed tempo changes, and checked any repeats. After a short break, the red light went on, and I launched into my first live broadcast as a conductor.

Not long before I began this conductor's apprentice scheme, a new principal trumpet had been appointed to the BBC Northern Orchestra. His name was Maurice Murphy and he had previously been a member of the much-vaunted Black Dyke Mills Band. Apparently, on his debut with the orchestra, Stravinsky's Ballet Suite, *Petrouchka* was on the programme. It is well known amongst orchestral players for its fiendishly difficult trumpet part. Maurice played it with such brilliance and panache that the whole orchestra turned to look at him in amazement, wondering who on earth this amazing player was. Maurice, typically, was blissfully unaware of its notorious difficulty.

George Hurst and I actually got on quite well, although temperamentally we were poles apart. He was a mixture of Russian and Romanian descent and could descend into doom and gloom. He would sometimes give me a lift in his car to the studio, reminding me that I was sitting in the suicide seat, his description of the front-passenger seat. One week, Mahler's first symphony was the main work, and in the car on the way to the first rehearsal, he gave me a miserable treatise on how he was going to purge himself. As it happened, it was during these Mahler rehearsals that I got to know Maurice Murphy. Towards the beginning of the first movement, there is a passage for three off-stage trumpets, which I was required to conduct. Maurice of course, was one of those trumpets, and in the long pauses whilst George Hurst was rehearsing the rest of the orchestra, we had plenty of time to converse. His support whilst I was in Manchester was much appreciated, leading to a mutual respect throughout his celebrated career.

After leaving the Royal College I had continued working with the orchestra I had originally formed in the College to perform student compositions. We met weekly at Queen Anne's House, the female hostel alongside the Royal Albert Hall, rehearsing as much of the standard orchestral repertoire as we could get hold of. We were an enthusiastic group, calling ourselves the Mercia Sinfonia, and once we felt ready we made our merry way to Cardiff to perform in the City Hall.

Alongside the main work, Brahms Symphony No. 4, we also played the *Welsh Dances* by Alun Hoddinott. He confessed to being quite amazed at the high quality of playing, and the mature, professional attitude on show. Like all of us he was particularly impressed by the virtuoso execution of the intricate xylophone solo in the finale to his *Dance Suite*. The soloist was a very young David Corkill, now regarded as one of the foremost percussionists in the UK and currently principal player of the Philharmonia Orchestra in London. Many of these players went on to hold posts in the major orchestras, and it is very gratifying to know that all this hard, painstaking work bore such fruit for all of us. A typical story was told to me by Jenny Caws, the oboist in the Mercia Sinfonia. She had been appointed Principal Oboe of the BBC Scottish Symphony Orchestra, and within days of starting work, the orchestra was performing Brahms 4 live from the studio. The conductor said to the orchestra, 'there's no need to rehearse, we all know this'. When the red light went off at the end of the broadcast, Jenny told me she gave up a little prayer, and silently thanked me for having learnt Brahms 4 so thoroughly.

I shall always be grateful for the enormous help I had from two of my fellow students at the Royal College of Music, both of whom lived at Queen Anne's House, hence the ready availability for us to be able to rehearse there. Jane Atkinson, originally from Nottingham, was first and foremost a violinist, but was also a highly accomplished pianist. She began her career with the BBC Radio Orchestra, a versatile group, now disbanded. She then joined English National Opera in the Coliseum, moved up to Glasgow to play with Scottish Opera, and finally to Cardiff, where she has had a successful career over many years, with Welsh National Opera. My other co-conspirator was Phillippa (Pippa) Thomson, a singer, who also had practical administrative skills, which were a huge asset to me in planning and organising our various rehearsals and concerts. Pippa sang in the Bach Choir, conducted by Sir David Willcox and became its secretary. Her organisational skills soon became apparent, and Sir David, who had succeeded Sir Keith Falkner as Director of the Royal College of Music, quickly appointed her as his personal assistant, knowing full well that her inside knowledge of the student life of the college would be an added bonus. I shall always be indebted to these two, and the success they enjoyed in their respective professions is testimony to their talent and dedication.

As a result of that concert in Cardiff, Hoddinott, along with the local press, particularly Kenneth Loveland, editor and music critic of the *South Wales Argus*, persuaded the Welsh Arts Council to give me a bursary to experience the everyday business and functions of a professional conductor. I chose the Dutch conductor, Bernard Haitink and the German maestro, Rudolf Kempe. Haitink had not long become principal conductor of the famous Amsterdam Concertgebouw, and was on the threshold of a glittering international career, making a fine name for himself with his interpretations of Bruckner and Mahler, steeped as he was in the enduring tradition and legacy of the Concertgebouw. Under the inspirational leadership of Willem Mengelberg, particularly his advocacy of the music of Mahler, the orchestra had become one of the world's finest, a status maintained by Eduard van Beinum and Eugen Jochum. Mahler himself also conducted his own music there. I spent a month with Haitink in Amsterdam, breathing in the atmosphere, as Haitink nurtured and cultivated this streamlined ensemble in this most impressive building with its sublime acoustics. Haitink was undoubtedly a superb conductor, intense in concentration, but unfussy and relaxed with the players, who revered and respected him. His beat and intentions were absolutely clear, thus avoiding unnecessary, tiresome, time wasting.

Haitink had also become principal conductor of the London Philharmonic Orchestra, and being with him and this splendid orchestra I saw at first hand the difficult working conditions of London orchestral players. Rehearsals would take place anywhere in London, in any hall available, and large enough to accommodate a symphony orchestra. A rehearsal in the Royal Festival Hall, for example, would take place only on the morning of a concert. World-class performances would take place despite these arduous, fatiguing circumstances, much to the astonishment of continental orchestras who could not believe the brilliance and resilience of British musicians. Unlike the full-time salaried players in the BBC and regional orchestras, London orchestras are self-governed, with decisions made by the players themselves through an appointed committee. The musicians are only paid on a work-by-work basis – no work, no pay. It's the responsibility of the appointed managers of the orchestras to secure engagements for the players – concerts, recordings and film work. If the standard falls, the orchestra's reputation suffers, resulting in a loss of work. It's an interesting philosophy, quite unique in the orchestral world.

Kempe was a completely different character. I spent time with him when he was in London, he having succeeded Sir Thomas Beecham as principal conductor of the charismatic Royal Philharmonic Orchestra. Unlike Haitink, who was early on in his career, Kempe came to London with enormous experience in the concert halls and opera houses of Germany, as well as the New York Metropolitan. Tall, commanding, with eyes that could bore into you, he dominated the concert platform. The players absolutely adored him, regarding him as the best conductor they had played under. I concur completely. Easily the best conductor I have ever seen or experienced.

Another outcome of my work with the Mercia Sinfonia came as a result of a concert organised in Hammersmith Town Hall. Unbeknown to me, a BBC music producer attached to the Light Programme, now Radio Two, was in the audience. I was eventually contacted and offered a date with a BBC orchestra. The engagement was with the BBC Midland Orchestra, a household name on radio, led by the equally familiar James Hutcheon. The broadcast was scheduled for the Third Programme, now Radio Three, and to my relief, I struck up an easy, workmanlike relationship with the orchestra. It was based in Carpenter Road, Edgbaston, a stone's throw away from the Warwickshire and England test cricket ground. This was pre Pebble Mill days – the BBC headquarters of its midland region, made famous by the live, lunchtime broadcasts from its spacious foyer. The building at Carpenter Road didn't appear to have the glamorous, modern appearance of its successor, but it had real character and was actually a Regency mansion, formerly the home of the Royal Institute for the Blind. I felt immediately comfortable, warmly welcomed, and made to feel completely at home during my stay.

The next engagement with them turned out to be a shattering event, catapulting me, with very little experience, into responding to a distressing, tragic incident. Having rehearsed as usual on a Monday afternoon, we all said goodbye, happy and content after a solid and productive rehearsal session and looking forward to the next morning's broadcast. I arrived to find an orchestra stunned and devastated by the most appalling, frightful news. On the way home from the rehearsal the previous day, James Hutcheon, the leader, and Peter Atherton, the young principal trombone, had been killed in a car accident. I felt a deep sense of shock as I had, in a short time, got to know them, but it was as nothing compared with the grief and loss of the players who had been their close working colleagues and friends, some for many years. The broadcast however had to go on, and with grim fortitude and tight-lipped courage, we completed our task. This was my first experience of having to persevere, whatever the circumstances, however tragic. These were the very memories that were invading my mind in Glasgow airport on the night of the calamity of nine eleven.

six
IN SEARCH OF
WORK

*I*N THE AUTUMN OF 1967, Jean and I decided to move away from the White City area. It had become very noisy, particularly at night, when pile-driving was taking place as a prelude to the building of the flyover on the A40 from White City to the Edgware Road. We rented a flat above a dentist in Preston Road, part of the Borough of Harrow, not far from Wembley Stadium. It was a short distance to Harrow Welsh Congregational Church which I'd attended on Sunday mornings as a student. The Reverend Eifion Powell, in the meantime, had been appointed as the new minister, and along with his charming, delightful wife, Rebecca, known to us all as Becca, transformed the chapel into a vibrant, buzzing place of worship with his inspirational leadership.

Jean and I both responded enthusiastically to his tireless dynamism, allied to a formidable, scholarly brain. Church history was his academic speciality, ultimately becoming its professor at Aberystwyth University, and then Principal of the Theological College. Eifion and I built up a close relationship, revelling in our intellectual debates, and the problems and difficulties in dealing with a church congregation. Like any organisation, the church is not immune from the exigencies and frailties of human nature. Fortunately however both Jean and I made long-standing friends in Harrow Chapel, not only enjoying their company, but also very appreciative of their support and encouragement. Jean and Becca, likewise, had become firm friends, able to confide in each other. Becca had the most endearing nature, a tower of strength for Eifion, and loved and adored by everyone. If ever there was such a thing as an angel on earth, it was surely Becca.

After much persuasion from Eifion and chapel members I agreed to become a deacon of the chapel. Perhaps in the same way as London orchestras are self governing, so nonconformist chapels are free to conduct their own affairs, with the deacons responsible for its financial and business matters. One could even say that the minister is its principal conductor and artistic advisor. Being a deacon, I got to know the members well, with all their foibles, quirks and eccentricities – the habitual strengths and weaknesses that typify any gathering of people. An orchestra is made up of just such a disparate group of individuals, but with one intrinsic difference – musical talent. This, combined with the pressures of intense public exposure and critical examination, creates a unique, incomparable fellowship, which I respect hugely and exult in being responsible for. That is my attitude and the way I have approached my chosen vocation, like the pastoral side of the ministry. I have no doubt that those early years in the warm, comforting bosom of my family, the Tabernacl influence under Myrddin Davies, my student years under such seasoned, healthy, tutelage, and the worldly knowledge gained as a deacon, moulded and matured me into the personality I am. It's no coincidence that although I chose conducting before the Christian ministry, my life is still very much involved with church life and worship, which has undoubtedly given me the resolution, strength and purpose, to survive and enjoy this extraordinary profession.

In Harrow chapel I came into contact with, and enjoyed the company of, so many diverse individuals. There was Haydn Thomas, tough and pugnacious, who thrived as the first Principal of the newly formed Uxbridge Technical College, and whose obstinate, stubborn dedication to discipline and educational excellence, achieved enormous success, the college ultimately being granted university status. His inseparable pal was John Lloyd, a surveyor by trade, but who had survived countless bombing raids in the Second World War as a navigator in a Lancaster bomber. He had also earned the special, unique badge, given to those who had parachuted into the sea. They were both rugby union aficionados and stalwart members of London Welsh, an affinity they shared with Eifion Powell as he, being tall and strong, had been a second-row forward in his earlier days. Eifion had a real knack in communicating with his congregation or in any public-speaking function for that matter, with a shrewd balance of the serious and humorous. If Wales lost an international match on a Saturday afternoon, you could guarantee that on the Sunday morning, he would arrive wearing a black suit and tie.

When we moved to Preston Road, the removal firm couldn't get my piano, a half-ton iron-frame upright left me by Dat, up the stairs to our first-floor flat. The piano was therefore left in the dentist's waiting room. After a while Eifion decided that I ought to have my piano upstairs, and organised a posse of men for the task. I was doing a week's work conducting performances of Sigmund Romberg's operetta *New Moon*, with a local amateur operatic society, and Eifion and his army of helpers arrived as I was leaving to conduct the show. Hours and hours later, having travelled to and from the theatre, and completed another performance, I arrived home to find them all still there, absolutely exhausted from their efforts, having failed in their mission. One of their number was Arthur Leaves, who was a dedicated asset to Eifion, especially in his untiring work running the chapel youth club. Arthur, arriving home very late, had to explain next morning at breakfast where he'd been the night before. When he said he'd been helping to move a piano, his son said. 'come on Dad, even I could have come up with a better excuse than that'.

In those days, the London Welsh Association had an annual December booking at the Royal Festival Hall to perform Handel's *Messiah*. On receiving an invitation to conduct, I suggested that for a change, they should try something different. They agreed, and Mendelssohn's oratorio *Elijah* was chosen. As a result of working with Haitink and the London Philharmonic Orchestra, I had got to know the players very well, and they all agreed to take part in the performance, albeit under the name London Welsh Festival Orchestra. They were, as you can imagine, superb. The role of Elijah was taken by the Welsh baritone Delme Bryn Jones, whom I'd first heard ten years earlier, singing in a performance at the Swansea Festival of my father's oratorio, *Dewi Sant* – Saint David. He was a coal miner at that time, and had been introduced to my father, who had recognised a glorious, natural voice. He emerged from a shift down the deep pit to make his singing debut. *Dewi Sant* was commissioned to celebrate the Festival of Britain in 1951 and given its first performance in the summer of that year in St David's Cathedral. I was present at the rehearsal and concert, and this was probably the first time I experienced that phenomenon of knowing the music already, it probably having entered my sub-conscious on hearing my father composing.

The *Elijah* performance at the Festival Hall turned out to be quite an emotional affair for me. Uncle John, with whom I had always had a close relationship, had died a month earlier. He had given me the bound, full scores of the oratorios he had conducted in the 1928 Treorchy Eisteddfod, namely, Elgar's *Dream of Gerontius*, Bach's *St Matthew Passion*, and of course Mendelssohn's *Elijah*, which I was using for this performance. I remembered Karajan's temperamental antics when I was refused entry to his rehearsal in this very hall, and my vow at the time that one day I would appear here. So, clutching Uncle John's *Elijah* score, full of his own conducting directions, I went to the banks of the River Thames at the entrance to the Festival Hall, and looked down with grim satisfaction at the same inky black waters.

Unfortunately, *cythraul canu*, that dreaded affliction, managed to permeate London. The conductor of the London Welsh Male Voice Choir was having an affair with the choir's female accompanist. One faction of the choir felt that this was bad for morale, as well as its public persona. Another faction felt it was a private issue, and nothing to do with the choir. Also, there was lurking the almost hysterically funny scenario of the accompanist's affronted husband taking the matter into his own hands and seeking revenge by jumping on stage in a public concert, and thumping the conductor. The inevitable result was a split, with an influential group forming a brand new choir, called the Gwalia.

In time, things settled down. The conductor of the London Welsh Choir resigned and left the country and the Gwalia began to become established, attracting new, young members. A composer, Michael Lewis, took charge of the choir, but at a key moment in their progress he was offered a big breakthrough, writing the music for a major film. I was asked to take on the choir. I didn't want a permanent or long-term commitment, but agreed to see them through a critical three-month period. The first task was to prepare them for a BBC audition, a hurdle that was successfully negotiated. Two concerts had been organised in Yorkshire, a fertile ground for lucrative and well-supported engagements. The first was in Pontefract, followed by a concert in St George's Hall, Bradford, a formidable test for the choir, and a hall that, unknown to me at the time, was to feature heavily in my future career. The final obligation was to successfully guide them through a Wigmore Hall concert, the famous London Chamber Hall, a venue synonymous with obtaining critical approval. Many years later, in various charity concerts in the Royal Festival Hall and the Royal Albert Hall, I combined the two choirs, hopefully to lay the *cythraul canu* ghost.

1969 saw the Investiture of the Prince of Wales in Caernarfon Castle. My father, now Head of Music at BBC Wales, was at the forefront of music planning for the ceremony, and often during this period, I used to drive him to Buckingham Palace for the many consultations needed in preparation for this momentous occasion. The investiture took place on 1 July within the medieval walls of the thirteenth-century castle built by Edward I, where the twenty-year-old prince received the insignia of the twenty-first Prince of Wales. The historic occasion was a television triumph, with a worldwide audience of 500 million, the largest TV audience ever for an event in Wales. Welsh musicians and composers were naturally heavily featured, as was the specially commissioned *Investiture Dances* by Alun Hoddinott. I was therefore very proud that subsequently my father was awarded the OBE for his services and contribution.

The Welsh National Opera Company, as it was then called, decided to honour the occasion with a special production of Verdi's last opera, *Falstaff*, the composer being almost eighty years of age at the first performance of his comic opera. An all-Welsh cast was assembled, virtually a roll call of the good and great of the time, prominent among them being Sir Geraint Evans, who had received much acclaim for his interpretation of the rotund, rascally, Shakespearean Falstaff. The music director of the opera company at the time was James Lockhart, and I, for some reason, was invited to be his assistant. It's still a mystery to my why, but maybe it was a political balance to the non-Welsh musical direction of the company. My first duty was to accompany James Lockhart to Bournemouth for rehearsals with the Bournemouth Symphony Orchestra, to make observations and provide notes on the development of the sessions for him. Originally called the Bournemouth Municipal Orchestra, a crisis occurred in 1951 because of a critical annual deficit, leading to termination of the players' contracts. In 1952, a plan to merge the Bournemouth Municipal Orchestra with the City of Birmingham Symphony Orchestra was avoided by an arrangement with the Arts Council for the orchestra to accompany Welsh National Opera. This production of *Falstaff* was to be their last appearance in this role.

Work began in earnest in Cardiff, where I sat alongside Lockhart as he rehearsed the singers, first musically, and then in production rehearsals. It soon became apparent that with such a collection of glitterati, trouble was not far away. To begin with, Geraint Evans had been made co-producer with John Copley, a very experienced, talented, opera producer with an established reputation. Geraint, although a fine opera performer, had no experience as an opera director, relying heavily on his earlier collaborations with Franco Zeffirelli. Copley was imaginative and full of ideas, with a clear vision of how to deploy the whole cast, the use of scenery, lighting, and all the special effects needed for a spectacular production. It didn't help that Geraint was a dark, brooding Welsh heterosexual, and John Copley an open and happy homosexual. I could guarantee that every Friday afternoon, after the general spats had built up during the week, there would be an explosion, and John would leave to catch his train for a weekend in London.

Another potential flashpoint was the fact that so many star singers were thrown together in the same place. Lockhart, quite rightly, was keen to establish his own authority, but by insisting before the assembled cast that an individual singer would sing things his way, whether it suited their voice and technique or not, he caused underlying tensions and aggravation. The Welsh National Opera Chorus was amateur in those days, with a deserved reputation for its exciting sound and rich sonority. It was split into two sections, one based in Cardiff, the other in Swansea. For each performance, only one group was needed, but a problem arose as to whether Cardiff or Swansea would sing in the performance to be attended by the Prince of Wales himself. There was a rather acrimonious meeting on stage in Cardiff's New Theatre after a rehearsal one night, exacerbated just a little by Lockhart challenging the men of the chorus to a fight. I quietly had a word in Welsh with the men, and the drama was diffused.

Apart from being a general dogsbody, doing all the fetching and carrying, my role, once the stage rehearsals and performances had begun, was to cue the singers and conduct anything that was off stage. As these were the days before closed-circuit television, I followed James Lockhart's direction down in the orchestral pit through any holes and cracks I could find in the scenery. I must admit, I found my involvement in the whole proceedings invaluable, instructive, and certainly revealing, seeing from within, and yet still an observer, the machinations and intrigues being played out before me. It was also a good and productive way to be involved with these first-rate singers, all of whom, in time, I would have the pleasure and privilege of conducting myself. Once the orchestra was in the pit I didn't have much contact with the players, but for years after I started conducting the orchestra myself the leader, Brendan O'Brien, a charming, engaging Irishman, would wickedly tease me about the copious notes I'd made right in front of his very eyes, in those first orchestral rehearsals in Bournemouth. Many of the players, on my visits to conduct concerts with the orchestra, vividly recalled the enjoyment of playing in performances of my father's opera, *Menna*. Commissioned by Welsh National Opera in 1950, it enjoyed much success in that decade with its haunting melodies, harmonies, and dramatic choral and orchestral writing. It has not been revived since, although I recently recorded the whole opera for Radio Three, to the astonishment and mystification of all concerned at its neglect.

I enjoyed our years in the flat above the dentist's surgery, the dentist himself being our landlord. My piano was safely ensconced in the waiting room, I'm sure to the amusement and bewilderment of the patients, and the garden was available to us in the evenings and weekends. The neighbourhood was a friendly one, and I felt peculiarly safe with Henry Cooper, the British heavyweight boxer, famed for flooring Cassius Clay (Muhammad Ali), living round the corner. His brother owned a fruit and vegetable stall nearby, his attitude typical of the cheerful, cockney warmth and relaxed atmosphere of the local shops. When we first rented the flat, the stipulation was no children. Jean was now pregnant, and although the dentist insisted it would be fine for us to stay as we had been ideal tenants for him, we decided this was the right time to bite the bullet and buy our own house. We bought a small, semi-detached property in Harrow itself, in a crescent leading off the road where I had first lodged as a London student. We had poured much of our savings into the purchase, and were rather taken aback by a surprisingly large, unexpected, solicitor's bill. With Jean now having to give up teaching, drastic action was called for and so I began working for a taxi firm. The saying goes that any experience is good for you, and I'm sure there must be some truth in it some-where, although often at the time it's not necessarily as clear cut and obvious.

The first day on the job I shall never, ever forget. My last call was a pick-up at a club in a hotel near where we lived, to take the client a few miles away to another area of Harrow – a nice, local job to finish, or so I thought. For some reason, my fare took a shine to me, and asked me to wait at his home and then take him down to some clubs in the West End of London. On our way to town, he confided to me that he had just been released from prison, had been celebrating in the club, and gone home to pick up what I'm convinced was the cash stashed away from whatever crime he'd committed. As far as he was concerned, I was to be his driver for the night. After touring some London clubs (thank goodness I knew my way around the roads at least) I managed, with a little persuasion, to extricate myself from a potentially extremely dangerous situation.

Times were hard, as work as a conductor was difficult to come by. It is said that working behind a bar in a pub is a most revealing exercise. I can unequivocally add that driving a taxi brings you face to face with every possible facet of life. At least in a pub, you are usually in a warm, friendly environment, but being a cabbie means you are out in the world, defenceless, in all weathers, faced with the best and worst of human nature. I had to do this for a few months, always hoping that I would get a long run, such as to one of the airports or a regular delivery of packages to firms in the City or deep in the suburbs. Looking back, I'm truly glad I did it, because it certainly revealed that there is a real world out there, broadened my horizons, and hopefully gave me an insight into humanity. It would have been much easier, with my academic qualifications, to have taken a full-time job in a whole host of areas, but this was not what the sacrifice was all about. It was to be a conductor – to live, think and breathe it. So, empowered with this dubious knowledge, I survived my unusual driving activity, and mercifully was able to contribute financially at a crucial time.

One day, to my eternal relief, I had a surprising, unexpected phone call. I had a great friend in London who was a producer in BBC Television, Geraint Morris. The son of the Reverend Gwilym Morris, a minister in a chapel in Gwaelod-y-garth, outside Cardiff, we had known each other in our younger days. He was a producer in an area of the drama department known as 'serials', and his present work was on the highly successful, long-running police drama, *Softly, Softly*. The main script writer was a hardbitten, cynical journalist, Elwyn Jones. Geraint had been called into a meeting to provide some input into a Christmas project for BBC 2. Elwyn had been commissioned to adapt a play, set in Wales, called *Choir Practice*, for television. The story centred around the problems created by a new conductor appointed to a choir, making his mark with wholesale changes – a new broom sweeps clean. This caused factions within the choir, those supporting the old guard, and those with the new man. The story was given added piquancy with a *Romeo and Juliet* sub-plot – the girl was a daughter in one camp, and the boy, a son in the other. Geraint rang me to see if I could join them in the meeting at Television Centre as there was argument and confusion over the music. On my arrival, Elwyn Jones launched into the problem immediately, asking if it were possible for the two factions to sing different hymns, which he named, at the same time, against each other. I said yes. He demanded how long it would take. 'A minute and a half,' I replied. 'Prove it,' he thundered. Out came the stopwatches as I began singing, and when the ticking eventually stopped with my completion at exactly ninety seconds, Elwyn Jones was satisfied.

After much discussion about the practicalities of recording such a play for television, I was asked to take charge of all the music. There turned out to be a great deal of it, especially as it was scheduled for Christmas Eve, and extracts from Handel's *Messiah* were needed. Glyn Houston, the veteran Welsh actor, was chosen as the conductor, and one of my tasks was to teach him some conducting movements. We met in a room one evening in the Television Centre. The casual observer doesn't usually realise how physical conducting can be, and after ten minutes of keeping his arms in the air, Glyn was absolutely exhausted. We had to adjourn to the bar, conveniently situated on the same floor, for refreshment and recuperation. For the recording, I used the London Welsh Festival Choir that had performed *Elijah* in the Royal Festival

Hall the previous year, and also the Verdi Requiem just a few weeks earlier, my first attempt at that wondrous work. Fortunately I was able to conduct the choir out of vision, behind Glyn, much to his relief, and the choir's, I'm sure.

Since our marriage, Jean and I had regularly visited Jean's mother, Phyllis, in Cardiff, at weekends. I had noticed a deterioration in her health, and now depression was seriously affecting her. On one visit, I found her condition desperate, for she had obviously given up the will to live. I just couldn't stand by and accept this, and so I invited her to come and live with us, as we now had our own home. She arrived the day before Christmas Eve in 1970. Jean had been to the hospital that morning, and the doctors had informed her that everything was still on course for the scheduled birth on 12 January, and they didn't want to see her again until at least New Year. I picked Jean's mother up from Paddington Station, and on arriving at our home even before crossing the threshold, she told Jean to go upstairs, have a bath and wash her hair, as the baby was coming. That night, Jean's waters broke, and Phyllis, that wise, shrewd lady, was proved to be right.

The snow began falling on Christmas Eve, after I had taken Jean into hospital. That evening, nothing seemed to be happening. Jean had discovered that the hospital didn't have BBC 2, and the play *Choir Practice*, my first involvement with television, was being broadcast that night at eight o'clock. The sister agreed that I could take Jean home for the hour-long broadcast as we lived fairly close by, but to return her immediately. The snow was now settling nicely, and as our house was down an incline into the crescent I parked my car on the top of the slope so as not to get stuck in the snow. After the broadcast, there was the hilarious site of Becca and me gently easing Jean up the hill to the car, and Eifion, the pack horse, following behind, carrying all the paraphernalia. He henceforth called himself 'Sherpa Powell', after Sherpa Tenzing, who had accompanied Sir Edmund Hillary on that historic ascent of Everest. Lisa Margaret was eventually born on Christmas Day, Lisa after the sublime Welsh folk song 'Lisa Lân', and Margaret, after Jean's sister.

Although reaching this far in my career had been quite a struggle, I was at least beginning to gain experience, and the next obvious step was to try to gain entry to a conductors' competition. After much vetting, I was among twelve to be invited to take part in the Guido Cantelli Conducting Competition in the famous opera house, La Scala, in Milan. Guido Cantelli was a hugely talented conductor, a protégé of the Italian maestro, Arturo Toscanini. After stunning successes, particularly in New York and with the Philharmonia in London, he was appointed permanent music director at La Scala in November

1956. One week later, at the age of thirty-six, he was killed in an air crash at Orly Airport in Paris. Being the first Welshman to appear in such a competition, I met Aneurin Thomas, director of the Welsh Arts Council, one lunchtime in a coffee shop in South Kensington, to ask if there were any possibility of financial assistance to get to Milan, and take part in the competition. He was very pleased that I had succeeded in winning a place in the competition, and readily agreed to support me at such a prestigious event, adding there shouldn't be a problem. Some time later, I had a letter from Roy Bohana, the assistant director of the Welsh Arts Council, informing me that I wouldn't be getting any financial aid, adding that as I was now a professional, I should organise my finances in such a way as to take in this kind of a competition. Aneurin Thomas rang me to say how sorry he was that I would be unable to go to Milan and compete. I simply replied, 'I'll get there, even if I have to walk.'

Family and friends rallied to my aid, Eifion and Becca being at the forefront of what everyone now regarded as a crucial crusade. I even had support from the choir at Hereford Baptist Church, where I had conducted some singing festivals. I arrived at La Scala, alone, to find all the other competitors accompanied by their wives or girlfriends, all subsidised and sponsored by their various countries. We had been given a list of orchestral works to prepare, ranging in style from Beethoven to Stravinsky. The opening proceedings didn't auger well for me, as in the drawing of lots I managed to pick out the last to compete, which meant a nervous, three-day wait before I conducted the orchestra of La Scala. To exacerbate the situation, the staff at the hotel which I had been allocated went on strike, so there were no facilities available. I managed to find breakfast – well, a cup of coffee and a cake, in a café opposite, and my abiding memory is of watching local businessmen drinking stiff brandies with their espressos on the way to work. Jean, at the request of the headmistress, had returned to teach for three days a week as her mother, Phyllis, was at home to look after Lisa. Eifion had become so anxious and perturbed that I was embarrassingly unaccompanied in the middle of such company, that he organised for Jean to join me. He went to see Jean's headmistress at Hammersmith County, and in his inimitable way, persuaded her to release Jean from her teaching duties for a few days. It meant Jean had to fly to Milan of course, but she didn't have a passport. Eifion took her down very early one morning to Petit France near St James's Park, which is where the passport office was situated at that time. After a six-hour wait, Jean was eventually issued with a temporary, emergency passport, and after collecting clothes from home, made her way to Heathrow Airport to be put on standby. She had never flown before, so I greeted a nervous wreck at Milan. One of the bonuses of my three-day wait was an invitation to attend a gala open-air performance of Tchaikovsky's Ballet, *Swan Lake*, played by the opera orchestra. It was an unforgettable experience, especially as the principal dancers were Rudolf Nureyev and Margot Fonteyn.

At last my wait was over, and late on a Friday afternoon, I turned up at the Opera House. I picked out an envelope from a number handed to me, and found it contained the title of the piece I was expected to rehearse and conduct. It was the first movement of Beethoven's sixth symphony, the *Pastoral*. Not speaking fluent Italian, I had been provided with an interpreter, René Leibowitz, one of the adjudicators, although I had already learnt it was wise not to talk too much in front of a crowd of orchestral players. The orchestra, of course, played really well, responding expressively to the sound and stylistic demands of Beethoven. Although naturally a nerve-wracking experience, it was an immense honour to conduct such an illustrious orchestra in those magnificent surroundings.

We were all summoned back at the Opera House at seven o'clock that evening, to be told the names of the three finalists who would compete in the closing concert. Time went on and on, and by nine o'clock there was real consternation and apprehension in the air. I am not in any way psychic, but every now and then I get a premonition, at times quite unnerving. It suddenly, and surely, dawned on me that I was somehow responsible for this long delay. It was therefore no surprise to me that when the jury eventually appeared, they announced that the three finalists were all Italians. My fellow competitors were absolutely furious, especially the one from West Germany, but on such occasions, I become quite philosophical. There was absolutely nothing we could do, and after they calmed down a bit, I suggested we all went for a meal.

The next morning, Jean and I strolled round the centre of Milan, relaxed now that all the preparation and hard work for the competition was over. Having organised our flight back to London we were attracted towards the magnificent cathedral, the Duomo. However I was also drawn to the second largest church in Milan − Chiesa di San Marco, Church of St Mark, where I had been told Mozart spent three months residing in the monastery in the early seventeenth century. I let my imagination soar as I imagined Verdi, a century after Mozart's visit, conducting the first performance of his dramatic Requiem inside those same portals. From a young age, I'd always had an instinctive empathy with Verdi's Requiem, and although naturally disappointed at the outcome of the competition, I took solace from my experience, knowing that this whole episode would prove to be beneficial. On the way back to the hotel to collect our belongings, we called in at La Scala to bid our farewells. One of the Italian finalists was just finishing his rehearsal, and as everyone was leaving the theatre, two of the adjudicators, René Lebowitz, who had interpreted for me, and Franco Ferrara, director of the Santa Cecilia in Rome, pulled me aside. They told me that I had been the cause of the delay, confirming my intuition of the evening before to have been correct. They explained that I was the complete unknown amongst the competitors who were already familiar to the organisers. They obviously had a clear idea who should be the frontrunners, and then I had turned up and apparently really upset the apple cart, and surprisingly, according to them, had actually emerged on top. It was quite amazing that these two revered gentlemen should have revealed so much to me, but they insisted it was so that I should learn and benefit from that knowledge. How wise. I returned to London with my head held high and with renewed confidence, to face what the future had in store for me.

seven
THE BBC
AND THE HALLE

FOLLOWING MY WORK with the BBC Midland Orchestra, I was offered dates with the BBC Northern Ireland Orchestra in Belfast. The ambience and people I met during my visits there, I found absolutely enchanting, no doubt fuelled by our Celtic concord. Then tragedy. The beauty and peace of that delightful island was shattered by the brutal killings and bombings. Before my very eyes, I saw people's lives destroyed, and nobody, and nowhere, was immune. One lunchtime, after a morning's rehearsal, I went for a stroll in the centre of Belfast where the BBC was located, to get some fresh air before the afternoon's recording. I was immediately aware of tension in the air, an indefinable portent. Even the military, on their routine patrols, appeared apprehensive and uneasy. At twenty past two, even deep in our basement studio, we felt and heard the unmistakable crump of an explosion. Adjourning to the canteen, we could see a huge warehouse across the road ablaze, with flames soaring into the sky high above us. After a while, when we realised we were in no immediate danger, I suggested we resume the recording, to which everyone agreed.

As I was getting more experienced, I was enjoying and benefiting from informative conversation and dialogue with the players. I was particularly at home with the mixture of acquired understanding of the old hands, and the unbridled, and as yet undimmed enthusiasm of the younger element. After one such convivial and informal gathering, when we were all relaxing following a fruitful session, I departed the BBC building, carrying a holdall full of music for the next day's recording. I had barely walked around the corner, when a vehicle drove on to the pavement in front of me, blocking my path, and within seconds, there was a gun in my back, and another pointing at my chest. I felt a slight tinge of relief when the figure in front of me opened his flak jacket to reveal an army uniform, but my ordeal was not yet over. They were very suspicious of the holdall I was carrying. After close inspection, and a search, I was cleared to go on my way.

Musicians have a dread of being late for any engagement, especially those working in London, with the everyday, chronic battle through travel and congestion, and not turning up at all is complete anathema. Yet such a horror happened to me in Belfast. Walking from my hotel near Queens University, I encountered a road block. The centre of the city was completely out of bounds, and it was hours later that I managed to arrive at the BBC. To my relief, the whole orchestra had been delayed, and the recording cancelled. Such was the wholly unpredictable nature of life in that city.

Having survived the testing grounds of those early BBC broadcasts, quite literally in the case of the Belfast escapades, I was offered engagements with the BBC Studio Strings. My father pointed out, rather ominously, that I was now being thrown to the wolves. They were a unit of tough, hardened professionals, brought together for specific broadcasting projects and activities. The last thing these players needed was a youngster lecturing and pontificating to them. They needed in fact respected musicianship and interpretations through clear conducting and guidance, not endless talk. This was the nature of the job, known as rehearse/record sessions. You rehearsed, then the red light went on for the recording, and the results were immediate. I discovered I was in my element in these highly charged, challenging situations, and I have no doubt that my rehearsal technique, clarity of conducting, and interaction with the wide variety of temperaments in an orchestra, were honed and matured by this exposure.

All these sessions took place in one of the studios in the BBC's Maida Vale complex. One evening a strange episode occurred which brought home to me, with ruthless clarity, the consequences of the demands and pressures upon musicians. During the recording of a particular item, I noticed that one of the violinist's bow was not actually touching the string. In the break that followed, I mentioned this to Reginald Leopold, the leader of the orchestra, and a formidable name in the world of string playing. His reply was surprising, not to say, astonishing – 'he must like you a lot. If his bow was touching the string you would be in real trouble.' The next day, the unfortunate violinist collapsed during a session and was taken to hospital where he was diagnosed as an alcoholic. Not long afterwards he was back in the unit, completely off the alcohol and, most importantly, demonstrating what a superb player he actually was. Over time I was to enjoy fascinating conversations with him, as

I now graduated into the next phase with this 'string ensemble'. Woodwind, brass and percussion were added, named on these occasions the BBC Studio Orchestra, mostly principal players from the London orchestras engaged on a freelance basis. This is where I first came into contact with the likes of Jack Brymer, a star clarinet player, revered by conductors and colleagues alike. Another was Maurice Murphy, that brilliant trumpeter whom I first became acquainted with in Manchester, now principal trumpet of the London Symphony Orchestra. Once again, collaborating with this class of musicians was having a profound effect, extending my repertoire, and also providing me with the first opportunity to conduct the music of Delius. At first I wasn't sure whether I was really understanding this dream-like, sumptuous music, or providing any real insight for the players. However when the likes of Jack Brymer took me aside and encouraged me to develop my interpretations of Delius it provided me with a timely stimulus to explore further the evocative, imaginative world of the composer originally from Bradford, but whose famous pieces were written during the last decades of his life spent in France. These recordings took place in the Aeolian Hall in New Bond Street, a building taken over by the BBC during the war years for recording concerts and recitals. I found its atmosphere very welcoming and comfortable, with its oak panelling and marble columns, and I am so pleased that I was able to perform in this iconic environment before its closure in 1975.

I was fortunate in that I had the support of a group of excellent producers, all fine musicians, some of them composers in their own right. Among them was Barry Knight, and his approach was to invite me one morning to a press showing in Leicester Square of the Western film, *Shalako*, staring Sean Connery and Brigitte Bardot. It was another little test to see how I would shape up, and after viewing the film, we went for some lunch to discuss ideas. Along with the other producers he was expected to provide music for different programmes, which I duly conducted. As time went on, it became very apparent that we were both buzzing with ideas, and wanted to create our own programmes. We had become aware of the paucity of broadcasts on national radio in celebration of St David's Day so we submitted a proposal to Barry's executive producers. To our surprise and delight, we were commissioned to provide an hour-long programme, to be broadcast live on St David's Day. The Pontarddulais Male Choir was engaged, and sensibly as it turned out, I went beforehand to rehearse the choir in Wales. Barry accompanied me, and we used our time to record interviews with various people for the broadcast on the significance of our patron saint. One such discussion was with Barry John, one of the most famous rugby players of his day, and star of the historic 1971 Lions' victory over New Zealand.

The broadcast took place in London's Camden Theatre, the home of the BBC Concert Orchestra, and this was to be my debut with this extraordinary, flexible outfit. The wise decision to visit Wales to rehearse the Pontarddulais Choir earlier, now became our saviour. The country was in the middle of disastrous electricity strikes, shortening our rehearsal time considerably in between the black-outs. Cliff Morgan, Barry John's equally famous predecessor as a Wales outside half, was the presenter of the programme. After his retirement from rugby, Cliff had forged an extremely successful career in broadcasting, having been noticed early on as a natural communicator, well able to vie with his great friend Richard Burton with his monologues and story telling. In the circumstances Cliff was the perfect professional to undertake this specialist role in our programme, although a little slip did occur, even possibly a Freudian one. The live programme began immediately on the red light, with the orchestra and choir performing, 'God Bless the Prince of Wales'. In the middle section I indicated a diminuendo, and Cliff began his introduction over the music, in his well-recognised, mellifluous tones. My name was to be announced as Owain Arwel, but Cliff, in his clear voice, announced it as Owel Arwain. The strange thing is, 'Arwain', in Welsh means, to conduct. We began the broadcast at eight o'clock, and barely were we off air, an hour later, than all the lights went out. We had been assured of the possibility of an hour's window, and an hour is literally what we got. The broadcast was judged a great success, and we all adjourned to the pub next door, where the landlord and his staff had provided candles to light up the bar. It turned out to be a very cosy atmosphere in which to relax and the choir serenaded us in the traditional, impromptu way of male choirs. The next morning Cliff flew to Europe, where he suffered a stroke. He was brought safely home, and with expert medical and nursing care, was mercifully restored to perfect health.

If conducting the BBC Studio Strings was akin to being thrown to the wolves, the next challenge facing me was potentially much more daunting. I had been invited by Clive Smart, general manager of the Halle Orchestra, to be the second conductor, alongside John Pritchard, in a performance of the fourth symphony by the American composer, Charles Ives. It required a second conductor, as so many sounds, rhythms and time changes clashed against each other. The composer was portraying the sensation of standing on a pavement as a procession of bands passed by, all playing different pieces of music.

The first strains are heard in the distance, a single band, then the conflicting sounds of those following, becoming a crescendo as they progress towards you, culminating in a deafening cacophony of sound right in front of you. Then, as they march away, the cycle continues as each band nears and then disappears. Fortunately for me, Clive decided to offer me my own concerts with the orchestra before that undertaking with John Pritchard.

My first concert conducting the Halle Orchestra was on 1 September 1973. Their rehearsal room was a methodist church in Moss Side, a dismal and dangerous part of Manchester. Apparently when Sir John Barbirolli first saw the high-rise flats being built he looked on in dismay, and prophetically announced that creating such a combustible environment would only lead to trouble. When I arrived for this first rehearsal there were guards protecting the players' cars, and patrolling the vicinity as we worked. I was greeted by the orchestral manager, Gerry Temple, a former commander in the Royal Navy, who took me to the conductors' 'dressing room', pointing out with reverence and gravity Sir John's battered chaise longue on which he'd relaxed so often in his final years with the orchestra. Gerry must have wondered who this innocent-looking boy was, about to face the unpredictable might before him, and so he proceeded to point out the potential pitfalls awaiting me. The leader turned out to be Michael Davis, whom I had previously observed as a fellow student, being auditioned by Sir Adrian Boult for the position of leader of the Royal College First Orchestra. The leader of the second violin section was Michael's father Eric, one of Gerry Temple's potential pitfalls, who actually turned out to be very supportive. John Adams led the violas in an easy, unfussy manner, in total control of his section, and the cellos were led by the venerable Gladys. It was she, a year or so later, who said to me, after the orchestra had been given a tour of a local brewery on a visit to Bexhill, 'Fear not, the Halle has great powers of recuperation.'

I began the rehearsal with my beloved Brahms 4. What a way to start one of the most defining moments of my career, as well as my life. The foundation for our eventual long and fruitful association was established in that first meeting, as we instinctively reacted to each other. I suppose it was obvious that in such an illustrious organisation someone would try me out, test me in some way. If anyone had tried it already, I was oblivious to it, although I think we were all too busy, caught up in the sweeping beauty of Brahms. It was while rehearsing the overture, *Carnival* by Dvořák, that one of the woodwinds teasingly, or was it wickedly, asked me where I wanted the pitch of a certain note. 'Bang in the middle,' I innocently but truthfully replied. The knowing, approving looks of the orchestra, indicated I had survived another examination, thanks to the experiences of previous occasions.

The concert itself took place in the Albert Hall, Nottingham, on a Saturday night. The soloist was the brilliant, naturally gifted pianist, John Ogdon, who had already won first prize in the Moscow Tchaikovsky Piano Competition, jointly with Vladimir Ashkenazy. He was a kind, gentle human being, and like many geniuses could disappear into a world of his own. Hence, on this occasion, he turned up at Liverpool instead of Nottingham, which meant that by the time John found his way to the correct city, there was very little time left for us to rehearse the concerto. This became an added test for me, as the concerto was Beethoven's fifth, the Emperor, a mighty masterwork which I'd never conducted before. The next day, the concert was repeated in the Pavilion Gardens, Buxton, with a change of concerto, Mozart's fifth, for violin, the soloist being Martin Milner, who shared the leader's duties with Michael Davis. This was again a happy and fulfilling experience for me, as Martin had been a supportive rock for Barbirolli, especially in his later years. I remember with affection visiting his home in the Derbyshire hills to rehearse the concerto, and I still have hanging in my study at home a framed picture of Barbirolli in pensive, conducting pose, which Martin gave me as a memento of our first collaboration.

I owe my introduction and subsequent twenty-eight year career with the Halle to the general manager, Clive Smart, supported by his indefatigable and irreplaceable deputy, Stuart Robinson. They were undoubtedly halcyon days, with an orchestra that had to be kept busy in order to survive financially. Clive Smart joined the Halle Concerts Society as secretary and general manager in 1958, having been an accountant with the firm KPMG, with the Halle as one of his clients. This information was of inestimable benefit to him as he knew full well that finance was ninety-five per cent of the orchestra's problems. Stuart Robinson, number two at the Buxton Pavilion, was soon co-opted by Clive as his own second in command, a perfectly balanced duo that was to work wonders for the Halle. Martin Milner started as leader of the Halle on the same day as Clive, and his number two seated alongside him, was Mehli Mehta, the father of Zubin Mehta, the Israeli maestro, who conducted the now world-famous tenor trio of Pavarotti, Domingo and Carreras.

When Clive started, he had to organise as many as 270 concerts and recordings a year, for the players to earn a decent living. He was also very aware that the players had no pension, because before the Second World War the Halle were paid a fee per concert, similar to the London orchestras today.

To try to supplement their earnings, there was an annual pension-fund concert, when the orchestra played for nothing. As a result, if they were very lucky, they might eventually get a pension of a pound a week. Clive, to his eternal credit, and financial acuity, established an annual pension plan for all the players, eventually creating a final salary scheme.

The principal conductor was James Loughran, who was the first to follow in the formidable footsteps of the fabled Barbirolli. I have the greatest admiration for James, as he took over the orchestra at an awkward time, and directed them with distinction for fourteen years. I, to my great advantage and development, was given the freedom, with Clive and Stuart, to compile my own programmes. This was of inestimable value, as I was able to build up a substantial, well-balanced repertoire, of symphonies, concerti and large-scale choral classics. Where else would I have had such an opportunity to appear regularly with a major symphony orchestra? The symphonies of Beethoven, Brahms, Tchaikovsky, Sibelius and Dvořák, became standard fare. Through accompanying the concertos of Mozart, Beethoven, Brahms, Tchaikovsky and Rachmaninov, I was introduced to the remarkable, established soloists of the day. My choral repertoire was enhanced with opportunities to conduct more unusual works such as Beethoven's *Missa Solemnis*, Prokofiev's *Alexander Nevsky*, Britten's *War Requiem* and Walton's *Belshazzar's Feast*. There are so many landmarks. I shall never forget my first performance of the *Planets Suite* by Holst, for example. It was in St George's Hall, Bradford, typical of the Victorian concert halls of the North of England, where only a few years earlier I had conducted the Gwalia Choir.

Accompanying concertos was an integral part of working with the Hallé, a concerto a prerequisite in practically every concert. The piano was the favourite instrument, followed by the violin, then cello, but the guitar also began to feature, mainly as a result of the growing popularity of Rodrigo's *Concierto de Aranjuez*, and the brilliant practitioners on the instrument, John Williams and Julian Bream. I first met the pianist Peter Donohoe when, at a very young age, he played a Liszt piano concerto when we were showcasing young, talented musicians. His own talent was prodigious and clearly evident even then, and a solo career beckoned. He actually auditioned for the post of timpanist at the Hallé, and emerged the winner, but Clive Smart, again to his credit, refused to give him the job, encouraging him to pursue the career that was undoubtedly meant for him. Years later, he appeared live on television, as one of six in the final of the Leeds International Piano Competition. After a sublime performance of Beethoven's Fourth Piano Concerto, to my astonishment, and that of many others, he was awarded only sixth place. Such is the lottery of competitions. His answer was immediate and typical. He entered the Moscow International Tchaikovsky Competition and, like John Ogdon before him, jointly won that most prestigious of prizes.

Another British pianist to win the Tchaikovsky prize was John Lill. Our paths first crossed unexpectedly within a couple of months of my Halle debut. I had been contacted by the management whilst performing with the Halle in Shrewsbury, informing me that there was a problem with the concert in Manchester in three days time. The outcome was I went home and learnt Rachmaninov's Third Piano Concerto. I met John on the stage of Manchester's Free Trade Hall before the orchestral rehearsal, to go through the music. I was quietly beating time, standing alongside the piano, when to my astonishment, John said, 'that's very good, most conductors are two bars out at this point'. I was sure he was joking, but thankfully I actually enjoy concerto accompaniment, which can prove to be an ordeal for some. While I continued my rehearsal with the orchestra, John had, without me knowing, contacted Jean, who was pregnant again and resting at the Midland Hotel where John was also staying. He said some complimentary things about the rehearsal and the young conductor he had just met, which must have been very comforting for Jean. This was an amazing gesture from a musician who had already achieved fame, and the resultant concert, my first in the Halle's permanent home, cemented a firm working relationship and friendship, which we both still value and treasure.

Geraint John was born in Harrow on 15 February, much to Jean's relief, who having had one child born on Christmas Day, didn't relish the prospect of announcing that her second had come into this world on St Valentine's Day. Sir Geraint Evans, with whom I'd had a cordial, growing rapport since those Falstaff days, expressed delight that we had named our son after him. My mother's brother, an area bank manager in South Wales also took pleasure in assuming the same. I never disillusioned them for, alas, he was named after my great friend, Geraint Morris. John, without any hesitation, was after my Uncle John, who, quite apart from my enduring empathy with him, had built up a close and supporting understanding with Jean. I toasted and celebrated Geraint's birth that night with Geraint Morris himself, Haydn Thomas and friends from Harrow Chapel. Those were the days when the stock of Welsh rugby was riding high. Initials were to the forefront, with J.P.R., the star fullback, and J.J. (Williams) haring up the wing. So we decided it would be G.J. scoring the winning try at the Arms Park.

Television entered my life again, this time an approach from the BBC's Music and Arts Department, based in Kensington House, Shepherd's Bush, west London. I was contacted by Herbert Chappell, who, already winning a growing reputation as a producer and director, had been recruited by Huw Wheldon, the formidable managing director of BBC Television, to contribute to the newly formed BBC 2. Before entering BBC management, Huw Wheldon had begun his career as a broadcaster, and it was as editor and presenter of the art's magazine programme, *Monitor*, that he made his greatest artistic contribution. Thus he was well equipped to assess the potential of Herbert Chappell. Bert, as he was known, had earlier made a name for himself as a fine musician and composer, writing title and incidental music for a range of television programmes and films, the most well known being the *Adventures of Paddington Bear*. Bert had become acquainted with my work with choirs, and proposed that I present and conduct an hour-long programme on the development of the English choral tradition. This, we decided, should not be done in the formal, documentary, talk to camera format, but that I would demonstrate, through rehearsing a choir and orchestra, how styles, techniques, and compositions had evolved over time. Naturally, because of my burgeoning relationship, the Halle Orchestra and Choir were chosen for these demonstrations. The programme began with excerpts from the *Messiah*, progressing through Mendelssohn's *Elijah*, Elgar's *Dream of Gerontius*, written at the threshold of the twentieth century, Walton's *Belshazzar's Feast*, and culminating in Britten's *War Requiem*. By rehearsing specific sections of these works, we explained the changing styles from the Baroque to the modern, and demonstrated the growing richness of the orchestral writing, through the liberating force of Elgar, and the complex dramas of Walton and Britten. It was an innovative way of describing musical, historical progression, typical of the televisual imagination of Bert, and the orchestra and choir responded enthusiastically to the challenge.

The second programme was a complete performance of one of the works we had discussed and analysed, Walton's *Belshazzar's Feast*. The orchestra tackled the technical difficulties of Walton's score with bravura, and the choir, as a result of the unselfish, thorough training by the chorus master, Ronnie Frost, was stunning in its precision, accuracy and conviction. The first performance of this dramatic, Old Testament oratorio, had taken place in Leeds Town Hall in 1931 as part of the Leeds Festival. Sir Thomas Beecham was director of the festival, but had allocated the conducting of the premiere of the work to Sir Malcolm Sargent. According to Walton, Beecham was convinced that the work was doomed from the outset, and in his grand, noble manner, declared to him, 'as you'll never hear the work again, my boy, why not throw in a couple of brass bands?' Walton, in his characteristic way, did throw in those extra bands, their added, antiphonal effects, an integral and essential part of any performance today. The critics unanimously hailed it a masterpiece, the finest choral work since Elgar's *Dream of Gerontius*. It was therefore a fitting conclusion to our television journey, chronicling the history of a long cherished tradition.

The Free Trade Hall was the location for the recording, complete with the two brass bands placed opposite each other in the balcony, on either side of the stage. Three weeks later, Walton made a rare visit to London from his home on the island of Ischia, just off the coast of Naples. Humphrey Burton, who had recently assumed the mantle of BBC Head of Music and Arts, Television, decided to take advantage of this happy coincidence, and invited him to take part in a studio discussion, as a supplement to the *Belshazzar* recording. As a preliminary, a lunch was arranged on the sixth floor of Television Centre, those present being Burton, John Culshaw, his predecessor, who had originally commissioned the choral project, Herbert Chappell, Walton, his Argentine wife Susana, twenty-four years his junior, and myself. It was a grim, miserable, embarrassing affair. The BBC hosts struggled to keep a worthwhile conversation, especially as Susana seemed to answer all the time on behalf of a very tight-lipped Walton. When he did eventually break his silence, it was with some devastating words, directed to Susana, but with the full intention of us understanding perfectly his meaning, 'darling, didn't we have to have an injunction the last time the BBC did something about me, in order to stop it?' 'Yes,' replied Susana, 'Lord Goodman dealt with it.' I was feeling distinctly uncomfortable, but far worse was to come. Suddenly, Walton interrupted the proceedings, and declared, 'I'm the only person who can conduct my music properly.' By now, I was doing my best to hide beneath the table and heaved a sigh of relief when it was time to leave the dining room.

Then, the strangest thing. Before going into the studio, I visited the gents toilet, probably the most natural function for any performer before going on stage, and discovered Walton there. To my bewilderment, he proceeded to tell me, as we washed our hands, that he actually found *Belshazzar's Feast* very difficult to conduct, especially the unaccompanied choral section before the final, crashing climax. This was a completely different Walton from the one I'd encountered earlier over lunch. Was it an act? Was he genuinely distrustful, or was it a wicked sense of humour? We adjourned into the studio. Burton sat in the middle, between Walton to his right and I to his left. Burton, speaking to camera, launched into his introduction to the programme, explaining to the prospective viewers, the details of the earlier recording with the Halle in Manchester, and that he had with him in the studio, the composer and the conductor, and that together we would view the performance. When we passed through the unaccompanied choral section that Walton had admitted to me he found so difficult, there was a thud as Walton hit the floor with his walking stick. Apparently he had been suffering from a little bout of gout. I looked across at him and, with a broad smile, he gave me a very reassuring thumbs up. The work came to its shattering, cataclysmic conclusion, and Burton, with no preamble, went straight for the jugular, and asked Walton what he thought of the performance. With tears running down his face, he declared it to be the best performance he had ever heard of the work. After about five minutes Walton interrupted Burton in mid sentence, saying he meant what he had said about the performance. After the usual refreshments and pleasantries, I departed for home, bumping into Walton, sitting alone in the reception area. Not only was he genuinely pleased with *Belshazzar*, but felt I had an instinctive, natural feel for his music, and asked would I take a serious interest in it. I felt very humble before this creative genius, and thus, with great enjoyment, have since spent my career nurturing and developing my interpretations of his symphonies, a large variety of orchestral music, concertos and choral repertoire.

A few years later, in 1980, I became conductor of the Huddersfield Choral Society, a story in itself, which I will describe later. It is relevant now because, on taking up the appointment with Huddersfield, I realised that the Society would be 150 years old in 1986, and I would definitely wish to commission a new work. I thought immediately of Walton, but remembered he had not been at all well, and had not written much music recently, and so I put the idea on the backburner. Then one night, having a shower, I had one of my strange, unexplained, prophetic experiences. I was thinking of nothing in particular in the luxurious warmth of the shower, when suddenly, I felt a strong presence of Walton. Believing it to be some sort of omen, I went down to my study and composed a letter to Walton. I explained about the Huddersfield anniversary, and my intent to commission. I admitted I knew he hadn't been well, nor written much music, but could he see his way clear to write a choral work, as long or short in duration as he wished, on any subject? I added though, that I had always longed for a setting of the *Stabat Mater* from him, words he had never set.

The letter was posted, and about ten days later, to my complete surprise, late one night I had a phone call from Walton from his home, La Mortella, on Ischia. He told me he still remembered that performance of *Belshazzar*, and all the performances I'd given of his music since, and he would certainly wish to write the *Stabat Mater*, starting immediately, emphasising that it was to thank me. I had a few words with Susana, and then Walton and I discussed the words, which are quite complicated. A definite agreement was reached and I agreed to his request to visit him on Ischia to advise and work with him as the work progressed.

Walton died early the next morning.

eight
FROM HONG KONG
TO LLANGOLLEN

T HERE IS NO DOUBT THAT to appear on national television in such prestigious circumstances was an immense stimulus to my career. The development of the English choral tradition, with specific emphasis on the strategic place of Elgar's *Dream of Gerontius* at the beginning of the twentieth century, had been the subject of my degree thesis. To put an academic exercise into practical realisation with such potent forces as the Halle Orchestra and Choir, combined with the full resources of BBC Music and Arts was an undreamed of luxury. Herbert Chappell was a master of his craft, with a fertile imagination, technical assurance, and a clear vision of how to present music on television. This, combined with the assembled musical gathering was pretty formidable, with the Walton in particular creating a dramatic impact.

I became involved in further projects with Music and Arts, including a performance of *Elijah*, recorded on a set specially created in a sports centre on the Heads of the Valleys road, north of Merthyr Tydfil. The choir was an amalgam of the Cardiff Polyphonic and Ardwyn Choirs, an excellent blend of fresh, young voices, and rich tenors and basses. I had particular satisfaction that the important baritone part of *Elijah* was sung by Benjamin Luxon, whom I first met when I was a novice on that BBC Northern conductors attachment scheme.

I had much pleasure in the creation of a television documentary, charting the development of three very different choirs, reflecting the male choral tradition in their respective areas. The mining community was represented by the Cwmbach Choir from Aberdare, Aberavon Choir represented the huge steel works around Port Talbot, and Trelawnyd Male Choir, the vastly different rural and farming district of Gwynedd, in North Wales. I relished the opportunity of giving a television platform to these honest, hardworking choristers, and one of the comments voiced in the film, I will never forget. When I questioned one of the young miners in Cwmbach on why he had chosen to go down the pit his reply was, incredibly, 'for security'. Those words ring rather hollow today.

The final programme was a performance of Cherubini's Requiem in D Minor, for male choir and orchestra, performed by the combined forces of the three contrasting choirs. The television presenter on that occasion in a church in Llanelli was Robin Ray, whose father, the comedian Ted Ray, had died the previous day. When I had a quiet, private word to sympathise with him, he showed great love and affection for his father, and took much comfort in telling me his father's last wish, 'to be cremated and ten per cent of my ashes to be thrown in my agent's face'. So typical, he said of his father's humour.

Meanwhile, my regular work with the Halle was developing well. Apart from the symphonies, I was also having the opportunity to conduct dramatic orchestral works such as Berlioz's *Symphonie Fantastique*, Rimsky-Korsakov's *Scheherazade*, Mussorgsky's *Pictures at an Exhibition*, and Elgar's *Enigma Variations*. I was also being subjected to critical scrutiny. This was a new experience for me, made even more daunting in that the two main reviewers were respected, distinguished writers. Michael Kennedy wrote for the *Daily Telegraph*, and was already highly respected for his biographies of Vaughan Williams and Elgar. Gerald Larner contributed to the *Guardian*, and had built up a reputation as a fearsome satirist; in fact, he could be quite withering. Thankfully I never suffered a lampooning. However when he began one review with the words, some are born great, some acquire greatness, others have greatness thrust upon them, I wasn't quite sure where he was heading, much to the amusement of the Halle management.

I don't think any performer enjoys the prospects of having the details of his daily work writ large in the newspapers and magazines. There are countless stories of dubious occurrences with critics, and John Lill often reminds me of being absolutely slaughtered in a critique when he wasn't actually the pianist in the concert. This type of unfortunate circumstance is hilariously portrayed in a Peter Sellers's film, *Only Two Can Play*. It's set in Swansea, and Sellers, with his unique talent and insight, manufactures a perfect Welsh accent, unlike most imitators who over-exaggerate in trying to portray Welshness. Sellers, playing the local librarian, is assigned to cover a drama performance in the local theatre, but he is diverted from his task by the flirtatious advances of a young blonde, none other than the delectable Mai Zetterling, and misses the performance. Undaunted, he writes an account of the evening's event. Unfortunately for him he discovers the next morning, emblazoned on the front of his own newspaper, a vivid picture of the theatre in flames, the performance of course, having been cancelled.

In 1976, the Halle Orchestra was invited to be the resident orchestra at the two-week Hong Kong Festival. Being the principal conductor, James Loughran was in charge of the first week's concerts, and I joined them for the second week. I arrived late one evening after a long, gruelling journey. There was no direct flight as there is today, and there were restrictions to flying over certain countries, necessitating lengthy detours. To add to the problems, we had to set down in Tehran for refuelling and change of crew, and then sit alongside the runway as the Air Force took over the airfield for some military exercises. The next day, sensibly, was free, and the Hong Kong Welsh Society had organised a lunch to welcome Emlyn Williams and myself to the festival. Emlyn was one of the leading Welsh actors of the day, well known for his readings of the stories of Dickens, which he was engaged to perform in Hong Kong. The welcome by the Welsh Society was especially friendly and generous, with the dining room of the hotel we were meeting in festooned with daffodils. The hotel itself was owned by a company called Hong Kong Land, and its chairman, fittingly, a Welshman. Nearing the end of the lunch, I leaned over to Emlyn, and whispered that one of us should say something in response to such a splendid feast. I suggested that he, being very much the senior of us, should do the honours. He began with the much-used, unaccustomed as I am to public speaking, ploy at which everyone laughed. He explained he very much meant it, as on stage, with the lights on him, he could only see part of the audience, wasn't used to addressing people, and promptly sat down. I ruefully contemplated quietly to myself, at least he faced his audience, while I spend my whole working life with my back to mine.

We adjourned later to a flat belonging to one of the members of the Welsh Society situated halfway up Hong Kong's famous imposing Peak. It was a typical Welsh, homespun, entertaining evening of storytelling and singing. Located as we were on a tiny island colony, the tensions with China were a very close and ever-present threat. The singing of the Sunday school hymn, 'Draw, draw yn China', translated as 'Yonder in China', now took on a particularly poignant meaning. It was probably the first time I was really aware of the true feeling and powerful emotion of 'hiraeth', longing for home. As I was rehearsing at ten o'clock the next morning for my first concert that same evening, I took my leave with the intention of having a sensible night's sleep. I needn't have bothered. My first experience of the insidious effects of jetlag had taken hold of me, especially the consequence of travelling eastwards, as seasoned air travellers gleefully pointed out to me. I would have been better partying all night in hospitable company. Instead, I tossed and turned sleeplessly in bed, alternating between wide-eyed wakefulness one minute, and peculiar, bizarre hallucinations the next. It was mind numbing, as at eight o'clock, when I got out of bed to prepare for my first rehearsal, I was fighting to keep awake. I'd been allocated the Peninsula Hotel on the mainland at Kowloon. This meant a journey across the incredibly busy waterway on the Star Ferry. I've travelled to concert halls in various ways, in all parts of the world, but never like that hair-raising boat ride, from Kowloon to Hong Kong. As it turned out, the concert went well, and the whole festival turned out to be a triumph for the Halle.

One of the characters of the Halle was a Scottish violinist, Jimmy Murray. He hailed from the Bellshill area near Glasgow and claimed that if he hadn't been given the opportunity to play a musical instrument at school and realise a natural talent, he would have had a life on the fringes of criminality. This is a classic example of the huge social benefits of providing musical instruments in schools, and the vital need for peripatetic teachers to train pupils. As it was, he turned out to be a lovable rogue, adored and exasperating in equal measure. In the orchestra, he sat alongside the leader, a position I find critical, not only because of the musical, personal understanding and empathy essential with the leader, but also the immediate and direct eye-line contact with the conductor. In Jimmy's case in the Halle, he had two leaders to contend with, completely different in age, playing style, and temperament. On the day we were departing Hong Kong, a Saturday, the flight was at nine o'clock at night. A school colleague of Jimmy's was an inspector in the Hong Kong police, and had organised to take Jimmy through the New Territories to the Chinese border. I was invited to go along with them, and after a few thirst-quenching stops because of the overpowering humidity, we arrived at a police post overlooking the border. All seemed so peaceful and quiet, but it transpired to be deceptive, as our host pointed out the positions of hidden guns and sundry military equipment to control the border. The atmosphere all around was unnerving and spooky, giving a stark, new perspective on the Sunday school hymn we had so recently sung with such innocent childhood memories. Being part of an orchestral tour our luggage for the return journey had been taken care of, and so on arrival at the airport we were greeted again by the Welsh Society, who gave an impromptu concert, the instinctive, natural calling card of any group of Welsh people. Then, to the astonishment and delight of the British Airways crew and passengers, we were serenaded onto the plane, to the stirring strains of 'Cwm Rhondda', Jimmy having been made an honorary Welshman, much to the mirth of the Halle Orchestra.

It had been a particularly successful trip for the Halle, who had been starved for some time of the opportunity of such an overseas tour. To add to the satisfaction, the Halle was the first British orchestra to be invited to the Hong Kong Festival, and when after take off the British Airways captain congratulated us all on our performance, and offered us a drink on the airline, our euphoria was complete.

It was the intention that I would accompany the Halle on a return visit five years later, but a phone call from the festival director changed all that. In 1980, the New Zealand Symphony Orchestra had been invited to the festival. They didn't have a principal conductor, but their Japanese principal guest conductor was causing all sorts of problems and difficulties, and would I ease the burden and share the concerts? I flew to Auckland, with a change of flight at Los Angeles, where the immigration queue at the airport was so chaotic, that although I had over three hours just to change from one flight to another, I had to frantically run to catch the Air New Zealand plane. From Auckland, it was a fairly short internal flight to Wellington, where the orchestra was based. The landing lived up to the description, 'windy Wellington', but after thirty-six hours of travel, I really didn't have a care in the world, and rested my head against a window as we bumped and shook our way into the capital. Just guess where my luggage was: still in Los Angeles, of course.

I rehearsed four different programmes for Hong Kong, with a day off in the middle for Waitangi Day, a national holiday. I had been contacted by a fellow student of my brother from Cardiff Medical School, whom I had met on my very first visit to Murrayfield for a Scotland/Wales International. She was now practising in Wellington's hospital, having married a New Zealand doctor. I had a pleasant, relaxing day at their home, basking in the warm temperature and the refreshing pool in the garden. Needless to say, having unwound a little, I woke up the next morning with swollen glands, an inevitable reaction to the hectic schedule. So it was off to the hospital where I was swiftly seen to by my newly found personal doctor, Margaret. That night, I had been invited to dine out with her and her husband, together with the manager of the New Zealand Symphony Orchestra and his wife, who was also a doctor. There ensued a scene in the restaurant that would have done justice to any of the Doctor series films with Dirk Bogarde and Leslie Phillips. Firstly, they seriously studied my symptoms, confirmed the correct diagnosis and the medication. They then promptly insisted that I take my pill with a glass of red wine.

We arrived a few days later in Hong Kong. The problem with the orchestra's principal guest conductor manifested itself on the first day of extra rehearsals. He had been allotted the morning slot, I, the afternoon. He protested that the morning wasn't enough for him, and insisted on going on into my time. This was not a good idea and psychologically unwise, as the players were plainly suffering chronic jetlag. The experience with the Halle had proved to us that we were absolutely correct in ensuring we did all our rehearsing before going on tour. Although he had been given plenty of rehearsal time and concerts back in New Zealand, my co-conductor just couldn't see the wisdom and prudence behind this common-sense approach. The result was a dreadful tension and atmosphere, and pure hostility and antagonism towards him. The inevitable consequence was that the first part of the tour, conducted by him, was marked by below par performances and poor reviews.

In the meantime, I had been contacted by Huw Pride, who had grown up with us all in Tabernacl in Cardiff. It was a surprising reunion and we enjoyed a Saturday night dining out, completely carried away with our memories and reminiscencs. Whilst I was in NewZealand, the local papers had been full of the upcoming England/Wales rugby international at Twickenham. These are pretty torrid affairs at the best of times, but the British press seemed to have gone out of their way to stoke up trouble, and magnify the bitter enmity. After our meal Huw took me to the Press Association to see if we could obtain the result, and we were informed Wales had won 8-6. I bade farewell, and returned to my hotel and rang Jean, delighted at the news. She replied frostily, 'Don't they play injury time in Hong Kong?' Dusty Hare, the England fullback had converted a penalty with the last kick of the game, to give England victory by nine points to eight.

Eventually, the day of my first concert arrived. We now had added, unnecessary pressures, as the orchestra was already feeling the strain of a difficult tour amid unfavourable reaction and press. The programme was all Brahms, consisting of the *Tragic Overture*, the violin concerto and the second symphony. Towards the end of the morning rehearsal, the orchestra became very agitated. They indicated that they were being distracted by my co-conductor who had not only positioned himself in the raised stalls right in the eye line of the wind and brass of the orchestra, but had proceeded to conduct behind my back. They were incandescent with rage, and I had to intervene to stop the trombone players inflicting summary justice. The programme was ideal for me, and

Dada as a boy at the piano in Arwelfa, c. 1920.

Uncle John and Dada with Nain and Taid, c. 1940.

Mama, Ieuan, Delun, Owain and Dada, in 1945.

Delun, Owain and Ieuan in the back garden of 1 Colchester Avenue, in 1946

Uncle John, Mam and Mama on the bench, with Dat, Owain and Ieuan on the ground, enjoying a picnic at Penarth Head in 1949/50.

Dada, Dat, Mam, Mama, Delun, Ieuan and Owain in Tenby, c. 1950.

Owain, Mama, Ieuan, Dada and Delun at
Barry Island, in 1952.

Captain of cricket at Howardian High School, in the league and cup winning year, 1955.

Howardian School Male Choir competing at the Urdd Eisteddfod, Lampeter, in 1959.

Mama, Owain, Ieuan and Delun on holiday in Hastings, 1961.

Jean's sister, Margaret, in 1962.

*Just married! With Jean outside Tabernacl Chapel,
Cardiff, on our wedding day in 1966.*

With Mama and Dada, in Dada's study, 1972.

that night, as if liberated, the orchestra responded magnificently, thoroughly deserving the standing ovation they received. The tour was saved.

For any fulltime professional orchestra, a tour, particularly overseas, is a very welcome relief from the daily routine of rehearsals, concerts and the essential, necessary travel to different venues. The Halle had a regular run of concerts. A Thursday concert in the Free Trade Hall would be repeated in the Civic Hall, Sheffield on the Friday, and a Sunday Manchester choral concert would be performed in Sheffied the night before. Sometimes a Tuesday concert in Manchester would be repeated twice again, and programmes would also be played in many of the northern towns, especially if they had large Victorian Town Halls. Bradford was a regular haunt, along with Blackburn, Dewsbury, Huddersfield and Leeds, with its tricky, reverberant acoustic. The Victoria Hall, Hanley, in the Potteries, had been a favourite of both Sir Thomas Beecham and Sir John Barbirolli for years, and I understood why. The acoustics were amazing, with its combination of vast height and space, and the unique sound quality as a result of the wooden surroundings. Unfortunately, these halls were not equipped backstage to accommodate a symphony orchestra, especially as they included members of both sexes, plus their instruments. The Halle is typical of the resilience of British orchestras, and throughout my career, I've been amazed at the high quality produced by these players in often trying and uncomfortable circumstances. Backstage at the Victoria Hall there was a passageway, slightly lower than the stage, that we all had to pass through. One day, between the afternoon rehearsal and the concert, there was an almighty storm, and this passageway was flooded. In order not to disappoint the expectant audience, there was nothing else we could do but paddle our way through nearly a foot of water. Such a glamorous business we were in!

It's quite remarkable for such a much-travelled orchestra that there were very few cancellations, especially considering the often difficult, dangerous winter journeys over the Pennines. Many of the players, some with more than thirty years' service in the orchestra, could only remember one or two instances of being unable to arrive at a destination, and that usually meant the local audience hadn't made it either. But not all the plans of mice and men come to fruition. For an out-of-town engagement, the Halle usually provided two coaches to transport the players, one pick-up point being in the centre of Manchester behind the Free Trade Hall. It is now the location of the G-MEX Centre, formally a train terminus, now a splendid edifice, often seen on television as the home of party political conferences. We were travelling to Northampton for the Halle's first visit to the newly opened Derngate Theatre.

Gerry Temple, the erstwhile orchestral manager, picked me up at my usual hotel, the Midland, and jokingly said let's see if the coach, whose departure time was well past, had left. We turned the corner, and to his horror the players were still standing on the pavement, complete with instruments, waiting for the coach to arrive. Coming from a former naval commander who had spent his life on the sea, the list of expletives is unprintable. His home was on our way to the M6 motorway and we called in to organise something to salvage the situation. The booking with the coach company was a regular one, and to Gerry's temporary relief the mistake was not his oversight. Two coaches were eventually promised, one for the centre pick-up, and the other for the second out in Didsbury, a suburb of Manchester, convenient for those living on the west side of the city. However, it would take another hour and a half. The coaches arrived, they met up, and made their way to the motorway. Then the next problem. It was raining of course, and the windscreen wipers failed to work so the coaches pulled into the motorway services for repairs. On eventually leaving the services, the clutch went on one of the coaches, forcing it to stagger its way to Northampton in a low gear. The full complement of players eventually arrived half an hour before the scheduled start of the concert. We had had no rehearsal. Through grit, extreme concentration, and inspiration, we made it. It was brilliant.

The Halle concert season in Manchester extended from September to May. For years, the orchestra followed this with a week in Harrogate, initially in the Royal Hall, and then in the new conference centre. The players stayed in the town for the duration, many of them camping in a field next to a Theakston's Pub, the Gardeners Arms. It became a tradition to have a barbeque around a massive bonfire, organised by the orchestra's tuba player, Stuart Roebuck. One day when I was working in Television Centre, I had a call from my producer friend Geraint Morris. He invited me to join him after I had finished, as he was hosting a reception for police inspectors visiting London to attend a conference. One of the inspectors I met was based in Harrogate, and he arranged for the whole orchestra to enjoy hospitality in their police club after our final concert. It was always a jovial evening as we provided free entertainment for our welcoming hosts, a sensible arrangement to have with the local constabulary. It was a shame when, due to financial constraints, the week in Harrogate was discontinued.

The next few weeks before the orchestra's summer break was filled with the Halle's own Prom concerts. Inaugurated in the 1950s by the conductor George Weldon, they emulated the concept of the London Proms, but without a promenade area. They were always very happy, relaxed occasions, an opportunity to showcase young, emerging talent, as well as presenting programmes in such a way as to attract new audiences.

The National Eisteddfod of Wales takes place annually, alternating between North and South Wales. A different town or region will put in a bid to stage it, and whoever is chosen in any particular year, appoints a chairman and a committee to organise the competitions, concerts and any evening programme deemed suitable. In 1977, the Eisteddfod was held in Wrexham, North Wales, and the chairman was a remarkable atomic scientist, Glyn O. Phillips. He approached me and asked would I organise the evening concerts for the week. This was quite an innovation, certainly courageous, as he felt that the quality of concerts each year, depending on the experience and imagination of the local committee, could be quite a lottery. My first task was to engage the Halle Orchestra. It was an obvious and welcome choice, considering its quality and standing in the musical world, my close working relationship with the players and management and, just as important, its proximity to Wrexham, avoiding excessive travel and overnight stays.

The first concert was a performance of Verdi's Requiem, with the orchestra joined by its own choir. It was a Sunday night, and as the all-Welsh rule didn't start until the beginning of the Eisteddfod proper on the Monday, we were able to sing it in its original language, Latin. The vastness of the wooden pavilion, as it was in those days, lent itself admirably to conveying the drama of Verdi's masterpiece. I had placed the offstage trumpets used in the Dies Irae high up in the lighting gantry, above the audience, creating a bewildering, chaotic effect to represent Verdi's vision of the Day of Judgement. The second concert reflected the Welsh love of male voice choirs. My father had composed a mass for male choirs, a *Mass for Celebration*, and close to Wrexham was the village where my father was born, Rhosllanerchrugog. The village boasted two male choirs, the Rhos Male, and Rhos Orpheus. But ne'r the twain should meet. They'd never sung together, a living testimony to the stupid, parochial jealousy that so often plagued our amateur music-making. I thought this was too good an opportunity to miss, and managed to persuade both choirs to join together for this special occasion, and sing with the Halle. The precision, richness and sonority on display was quite extraordinary, and made one wonder why it could not have been done before. Funnily enough, the Eisteddfod was again in Wrexham in 2011 and I managed to get the two choirs together again to sing my father's stirring hymn, 'Tydi a Roddaist', for a BBC2 television documentary. I'm all for healthy competition, but co-operation can reap huge dividends as well. The result, as before, was stupendous, and the joy on the faces of the men at their achievement was a delight to behold.

The next concert in the 1977 Eisteddfod was a performance of Beethoven's *Missa Solemnis*, one of the great choral classics. It is fiendishly difficult, with huge physical, technical and musical demands on the choristers, faced with the profundity of Beethoven's compositional maturity. The choice of work was a request from the music committee, a real challenge for the Eisteddfod choir, formed specially for this one event. Earlier in the Halle season, I had performed the *Missa Solemnis*, and suggested that the Halle Choir augment the Eisteddfod choir, to which they readily agreed, having now realised the mammoth task ahead of them. I applauded the courage in choosing such a challenging work, and they diligently set about their endeavours under the training of a local schoolteacher, Mair Carrington. Due to the all-Welsh rule, the words of this magnificent setting of the ancient Latin mass had to be translated, and sung in Welsh. Mair, to her eternal credit, travelled regularly to Manchester to teach the Halle Choir to sing in Welsh. The sight and sound of a large group of Mancunians and Lancastrians singing in Welsh was something to behold, and never to be forgotten, and they talked about it for years afterwards.

I do wonder how on earth singing the great Latin choral classics or Italian arias in Welsh can be be the saviour of the Welsh language. I'm a fluent Welsh speaker, an avid supporter of the language and encourage its use. I'm glad that professional programming and output of S4C, the Welsh-language Channel 4, has been quite exemplary. It has reached all corners of Wales and beyond, appealing to all ages through broadcasting and commentating in Welsh on everyday pursuits such as sport, pop, literature, music, news, arts, drama, soaps, and documentaries on a vast array of subjects. The difficulty with translations is that there is always a problem fitting the words to the music, not to mention the delicate sounds and accents created by the composer setting the original words. I respect enormously the poets in Wales and the talent, intellect and scholarship of the bards, but I am sure they would be the first to acknowledge they know very little of the parallel intricacies of music. As musicians, we have a strong desire, indeed a duty, to present music to the highest possible standard, but being encumbered with awkward translations severely restricts our capabilities and choice of repertoire.

Perhaps education has been a problem over the years. When I was in school, I and my contemporaries in south Wales would be given a choice between learning Welsh or French. If you were considered bright, Latin came before Welsh, and Welsh was often reduced to the same status as needlework. One could even suggest that today every pupil should be taught Welsh beyond current curricular requirements. I have spent a great deal of time in Sweden, Denmark and Finland. These countries are proud of their languages, and it would be unthinkable if they weren't their respective first languages. They also learn English in schools, and the television in their homes bombards them with British and American programmes, untranslated. Yet they still protect their own language, and profess amazement to me that Wales, a country they have a great deal of affection for, can't do the same. The final concert in that 1977 Wrexham Eisteddfod included a performance of Prokovief's *Peter and the Wolf.* The narrative alongside the music was in Welsh. It was most appropriate and fitted perfectly.

I enjoyed the variety of workload and the challenge of contrasting halls which I experienced with the Halle. The players seemed to take it all in their stride, with humour and good spirit. Sometimes things didn't turn out quite to plan. One such occasion was a visit to Warrington. Eyebrows were quizzically raised as to why we should visit this particular town, but on arrival we found a festival taking place with some interesting participants, including Johnny Dankworth and Cleo Lane. Things did not start very well, as halfway through the afternoon rehearsal, the fire alarm went off in the hall. It didn't just go off, it was deafening, the attack on the ears excruciating. The result was the hilarious sight of eighty personnel, complete with an array of musical instruments, outside in the pouring rain in the middle of the street.

However, further hysteria and improbable antics were to follow. The hall was typically Victorian, with a large organ at the back of a steeply raised stage. The organ was being refurbished, covered with scaffolding and tarpaulin. The woodwind, therefore, were situated behind the strings in front of this monstrosity, while the brass were placed high to the right-hand side of the organ, and the timpanist, alone, separated from everyone, to the left of the organ. The main work in the second half of the concert was Beethoven's sixth symphony, the *Pastoral.* I noticed the timpanist, for comfort, sitting on a chair behind his set of timpani, instead of the high stool used in performance, as he had about half an hour before he actually played. We started the symphony with its lilting, gentle melody and I noticed that the timpanist had closed his eyes. I started the second movement with its lugubrious description of a slow-moving stream, and as it proceeded dreamily on, the timpanist fell fast asleep, his chin resting gently, deep into his chest. I was now really in trouble, because the next movement, the scherzo, goes straight without a break into the storm.

Normally, the set of timps would be placed amongst the brass, and anyone could have easily woken the timpanist. However because he was alone, high at the back of the stage, with the organ repairs a barrier between him and the players, no one could see him, nor be aware of his predicament. The timpani, of course with its thunderous outburst, is absolutely essential. The Halle had two orchestral assistants who drove the orchestral van carrying all the large instruments, stands, and baskets full of music for our various performances. They were both called Les, and one of them during a concert has to be dressed in a dinner jacket and black tie when they are on the stage making any necessary adjustments. Les No. 1 was on duty that night, and when I came to the end of the slow movement with the timpanist still deeply asleep, a door opened halfway up the stage on my left, the same side as the timpanist. The figure of Les appeared. He looked down at me, up at the sleeping figure and back at me. I nodded, indicating he should get up there. He slowly crawled up the steps in full view of the audience, who were now well aware of the unfolding crisis. Les reached the offending player and tapped him on the knee. As he woke with a start, the audience let out a huge, collective, hurray.

nine
OUTSIDE
BROADCASTS

*O*UTSIDE BROADCASTS HAS BEEN an integral part of the BBC since it was formed in 1922. The initial broadcasts were on radio, and it was not until 1937 that the first television outside broadcast took place – the Coronation of King George VI, but only the procession was shown, as the ceremony inside Westminster Abbey was considered too sacred for the intrusion of television cameras. My first connection with the BBC's Outside Broadcast department was through Cliff Morgan. Since his recovery from his stroke, he had joined the executive ranks of the BBC, becoming Head of Outside Broadcasts, Television. Outside Broadcasts was known as a group which split two ways, sport with its own head of department, and events, also with its own head, responsible for anything from the Coronation to *Mastermind* via *One Man and his Dog*. 1977 marked the Silver Jubilee of Queen Elizabeth II's ascension to the throne. Cliff decided that it should be celebrated in fine style, and asked me, together with the producer/director John Vernon, to come up with something spectacular. John was an experienced member of the Outside Broadcast team, having cut his teeth directing galas in Glyndebourne and Covent Garden, and, being a sailor himself, had made the Oxford and Cambridge boat race, with its unpredictable nature and weather, and multi-camera demands, his speciality. To reflect Cliff's grandiose vision, John and I set about forming a choir representative of the United Kingdom. It eventually numbered 550, made up of groups in northern and southern England, Scotland, Wales and Northern Ireland. Before any choral concert, I always rehearse the choir alone, in their own rehearsal room, for them to get to know me, and I to know them as individuals. I've always found this extremely helpful, in fact essential, to obtain a high level of musical co-operation and understanding. For such a musical extravaganza, there was of course only one venue, the Royal Albert Hall. The visual spectacle was stunning, and the occasion was given added gravitas by the stentorian tones of the actor Robert Hardy, in his presentation of the event. A choral medley had been specially composed, deploying tunes and airs typical of the four nations. Before conducting the two-and-a-half-hour live broadcast, I was charged with rehearsing the audience in this medley. In one sense it was quite nerve-wracking, as the strict time discipline of a live broadcast was looming, but it proved to be well worthwhile, as the sound of an audience of 5000, plus the choirs, singing in complete harmony, left an indelible, abiding impression on all those in the hall, and watching at home.

Little did I know how this one event, particularly my rehearsing the audience, was going to influence my career so dramatically. Following the success of the Jubilee concert, Cliff Morgan and his fellow executives decided they wanted a live Christmas Eve concert, which I would present, as well as conduct. They had apparently been impressed with the way I communicated with the audience in teaching them the medley, and so they saw a further potential in me. The setting chosen for this Christmas celebration was the Central Methodist Hall just across the road from Westminster Abbey. The BBC Concert Orchestra once again provided superb accompaniment, with the Royal Choral Society in full voice in the *Messiah* Christmas choruses, and the catchy arrangements of Christmas carols by the veteran of radio music, Robert Docker. One of the highlights of the programme was the final scene of the first act of Puccini's Opera *La Bohème*, set appropriately in an artist's studio on Christmas Eve. The sequence featured the well-known arias, 'Che gelida manina', 'Your tiny hand is frozen', 'Mi chiamano Mimi', 'they call me Mimi', and ended with the duet, 'O soave fanciulla', 'Lovely maid in the moonlight'. Although often sung at today's popular concerts, it was unusual then to have such a long sequence programmed, so we might have begun a trend.

Presenting the programme was a daunting challenge for me There was no autocue and between musical items I would have to aim at a camera, sometimes some distance away, watch out for the red light on the side of the camera indicating that it was the one taking the picture, and deliver my introduction. This television broadcast seemed to have struck a chord with the viewers, which was not lost on the BBC hierarchy. There was now talk of a series, and although I was completely ignorant of it, there was much tooing and froing between the various departments as to who would take the plunge. The offer came from the Outside Broadcast group, naturally under the auspices of the events department, and thus the long-running series, *The Much Loved Music Show*, was born. John Vernon was to be the producer/director, and the brief was to present programmes from the various concert halls around the country featuring the symphony orchestras of the different regions – Birmingham, Bournemouth, Liverpool, Manchester, Glasgow and Cardiff. The series became very popular, often being the subject of viewers' points of view. In many ways the recipe was quite simple, descriptive orchestral items, a variety of singers in excerpts from opera, movements from concertos, and choirs singing highlights from opera and oratorio. It proved there was a love and need for classical music, and I've been assured by countless people, the public and professionals alike, that we not only popularised classical music, but opened the eyes and ears of many to its abundant riches and hidden treasures. I am told that a happy consequence of this exposure was to increase the numbers attending live concerts, a timely boost for orchestras struggling to maintain audiences.

My collaboration with Outside Broadcasts led directly to an event that was to give me much personal pleasure and satisfaction. In 1969 I had watched the Investiture of the Prince of Wales on television in our flat above the dentist's, and I remembered how proud I was of my father's involvement in that historic ceremony. For me, those were the days of struggle, which I have never, ever forgotten. Now, ten years later, it was decided to commemorate that anniversary. John Vernon and I, because of our growing reputation in organising large-scale spectaculars were given the honour of compiling a suitable celebration. We decided it was practically impossible to replicate the grandeur and magnificence of the Royal ceremonial a decade earlier. However, we still had the magnificent Caernarfon Castle and, using the orchestral and choral forces at our disposal, together with a number of soloists, we were able to utilise every nook and cranny, every niche and cavity, to display the magnificence of the surroundings, and project the music to great effect. To crown the occasion, the Prince of Wales took part in the proceedings with poise and dignity, positioned on the slate circle where he had stood to be invested by his mother, Her Majesty the Queen.

Outside Broadcasts, along with Music and Arts, Features and Sport was based in Kensington House, a vibrant hub of creativity. It had its own bar, which was a relaxing meeting place at the end of a day of planning. All the departments mixed freely, exchanging ideas and adding fresh input into each other's myriad projects. Features was a department whose output included documentaries and shows on consumer subjects, as well as those exposing malpractice and injustice in society. The head of the department was Desmond Willcox, and it was his wife, Esther Rantzen, who fronted many of these programmes, making an enormous contribution through her fame and reputation, to championing people's causes. One of Esther's ideas was to spotlight different and unusual professions. To demonstrate this, she invited members of the public to write in, volunteering to attempt an ambition they longed to achieve. The series was given the title, *The Big Time*. Inevitably, someone requested to conduct an orchestra, and I was asked by Esther whether I would mentor this individual, so he could eventually conduct an orchestra.

I must admit I had my qualms about the whole thing. When I had my first major television success with the English choral project and Walton's *Belshazzar's Feast*, I was taken out for lunch by another producer in Music and Arts, Ian Englemann, nephew of the venerable news and current affairs broadcaster, Franklin Englemann. This was the joy of working in Kensington House, because as we all intermingled regularly, Ian was well aware of my work for his own department. He, in the most friendly, fatherly way, advised me to be very careful for a while and discriminate wisely, as I was very likely, according to him, to be deluged with television work. Television, he said, could be a cruel mistress, eating you up and spitting you out. They were shock tactics, but I felt very humble that he should bother to give me the time to share his concerns. These graphic words now rang loud and clear as I contemplated Esther's proposition. The director for the programme was a hugely talented, visionary young man, Ian Sharpe, whom I'd already met in the general mêlée at Kensington House. I voiced my concerns to him, so he and his wife came out to our home in Harrow one Saturday night to thrash out the potential problems and pitfalls. After many hours, he promised he would look after me and protect me, as he knew better than anyone that Esther was a formidable lady, and could be very persuasive. Having firmly established my role, and decided how we would approach the challenge, I agreed. By a strange coincidence, I had a phone call the next morning from a very prominent, high-profile executive at the BBC, funnily enough, not in Features but in another department. I was advised I would never appear again on BBC television if I didn't agree to do *The Big Time*. I took a deep breath, counted to ten, and calmly informed him that I had already agreed to take part.

By this time my television activities were not the exclusive reserve of the BBC. Southern Television, based in Southampton, had an extremely enlightened chairman, who adored music, and arranged for his company to televise two operas a year from Glyndebourne. A young employee of Southern

Television, Dave Heather, was beginning to make his mark as a director. Having begun his career as a cameraman, he was well versed in the technicalities of television, as well as in the endless, visual possibilities at his disposal. Armed with the knowledge of his chairman's desire to project music on the small screen, he approached the general manager of the Bournemouth Symphony Orchestra, Ken Matchett, to ask whether he would be interested in the orchestra being involved in a series of music programmes. Although Dave had an inkling that the orchestra had financial problems, he was just a little surprised that Ken Matchett appeared less than enthusiastic, asking for time to check the orchestra's list of engagements, and its availability to undertake such a commitment. He obviously did not wish to reveal or admit to the orchestra's dire financial circumstances.

An agreement was reached, and the result was an extremely successful series, with the tantalising title, *Music in Camera*. It was a half-hour programme, transmitted immediately following ITN's flagship, *News at Ten*, which was created by the Welshman, David Nicholas, later knighted for his contribution to broadcasting. Although late at night, it was a perfect slot. I was not involved in the early programmes, but when Dave Heather called me to see whether I was interested in his new venture I saw it as a perfect vehicle for exposing a wide public to the fulfilment derived from music. I have always believed, and still firmly do, that music should be available for everyone to enjoy its ageless melodies and endless beneficial properties. People often tell me, even good friends, that they don't go to concerts or listen to classical music, because they don't know anything about it or understand it. I reply by saying that it's my responsibility and that of other trained musicians to try to comprehend and unravel the mysteries of music. My enjoyment and gratification therefore comes from making music accessible to everyone of all ages. You are never too young, nor too old.

The series itself grew in stature, with high audience ratings. Being studio based, Dave was free to give reign to his directorial talent, with clever, but appropriate lighting effects, and intimate, ingenious close-ups of performers, which in itself made for good, attractive television. We were fortunate to have, over the years, a galaxy of soloists, including singers and pianists, violinists and cellists, and even a brilliant, highly attractive recorder player. One recording the orchestra never forgot was the day they supplemented their fee with overtime payments. One soprano had not particularly endeared herself to the orchestra with her fussy, snooty attitude towards them. There was an agreed orchestral time set aside for the day's session, known as a four over five, which meant a three-hour rehearsal, a one-hour break for refreshment, and changing into the appropriate dress code, and an hour for recording. We rarely, if ever, went into overtime, as it necessitated extra payment for every additional seven minutes. However, as if the gods had willed it, and to the ecstasy of the orchestra, our 'star soprano' on the recording just couldn't get things right. The overtime clock ticked on and on, and for once, the orchestra didn't mind staying on. Thereafter the orchestra wickedly and mischievously renamed our sessions by the singer's name.

One particular day stood out above all others, and was still talked about for years afterwards, the reason being, mercifully this time, musical and emotional. Dave and I had become not only close friends, but equally committed to presenting music in an exciting, approachable manner. There was so much fine music we could present, and by reflecting so many different tastes in music we believed we could open up new horizons. Because of my intimate knowledge, not to say my deep affection for the unique sound of Welsh male voice choirs, we invited the Cwmbach Male Choir to perform with the Bournemouth Symphony Orchestra in one of our programmes. I had earlier invited the Cwmbach Choir to join me at the Belfast Festival. The concert there on the Saturday night was as powerful a rendition of male choral singing you could experience anywhere in the world. In that strife-torn city, the audience, suffering such untold misery, and facing daily danger, released their pent-up emotions in rousing, thunderous approval. The sight of those tough, hardened, mining community men, with tears streaming down their faces, is still etched firmly, and forever in my memory. The assistant director of the festival, Betty Craig, had been unable to attend the concert which she had worked so tirelessly to organise, especially in transporting a male choir from Wales in such treacherous times. She had been injured in a bomb blast and hospitalised as a result. The day after the concert, without her knowledge, I had arranged for a large, double-decker bus to transport the choir to the hospital. I went alone to her room, and with the help of a nurse, manoeuvred her into a wheelchair, on the pretence that she needed some fresh air. Her look of astonishment and disbelief when she came face to face with the Cwmbach Choir was blissful to behold, and the choir approached this private appearance as if they were performing before an audience of thousands.

With the profound impression of the Belfast episode still fresh in my mind, I had every confidence that we had the prospect of a very fine contribution to the *Music in Camera* series. It was in the rehearsal that I was aware that something unusual was happening. The orchestra was visibly moved and inspired by a sound they'd obviously not confronted before. Likewise, the camera crew and technicians were transfixed, and even the usual ebullient Dave Heather was reduced to silence in the control room. News of the happening in the rehearsal must have got around, for by the time we came to record, every free space in the studio was crammed with personnel from different departments, and even the canteen ladies were there. Needless to say, the recording was a stunning success, and ultimate proof of my conviction that it is possible, with the right exposure, to open people's hearts and minds to the magic of music.

Choral music has been an intrinsic part of my life. From those tentative, first steps in Tabernacl chapel, through those youthful conducting days in school, chapel and university, singing, in all its forms, has been inextricably linked to my career. There is not a shadow of doubt that actually singing in choirs themselves gave me a clear understanding of the demands on choristers, in pitch, breathing, projection and the necessity for perfectly balanced ensemble. This grounding has been fundamental in my approach to the conducting of choirs, and has given me gratification, thrills and excitement that it's almost impossible to express. To begin with, the combination of what I consider to be the two finest sounds in the world, a symphony orchestra and a full-blooded choir, is unbeatable. Add to this the fact that many of the world's greatest composers have written some of their finest creations for these combined forces, the ultimate challenge is laid before you.

Following those early experiences in the Royal Festival Hall with the London Welsh Festival Choir, it's no coincidence that my development and progress as a choral conductor was cemented with my activities with the Halle. Its choir was a revelation, scrupulously auditioned, and thoroughly professional in its attitude, as befits an organisation such as the Halle. The chorus master, Ronnie Frost, a church organist and choir master, was equally professional, and ruthlessly thorough in his preparations. He was engaged as a chorus master, and that, simply, was what was expected of him, no histrionics or climbing above one's station, but to train the choir to perfection. It could then be handed on to the conductor, be it Barbirolli, Loughran or any guest conductor like myself, who would put them together with the orchestra, interpret the music, and perform the chosen work in the concert.

This business-like attitude bore huge dividends, and so I began a fruitful, mutually satisfying relationship with the Halle Choir. My first choral work with the choir was very unusual, and rarely performed – it was the First Choral Symphony by Gustav Holst, a performance to mark the centenary of his birth. Like Walton six years later, it was commissioned by the Leeds Festival in 1925.

Holst chose his words from the poems of Keats, the most well known being the 'Ode on a Grecian Urn'. There was a fruitful, reciprocal arrangement with the Sheffield Concerts Society, and for choral performances, the Halle Orchestra would be joined by the Sheffield Philharmonic Choir. They again were thoroughly rehearsed, and it was always very satisfying to be able to repeat choral works, especially one as rare as the Holst.

There was always an annual Halle *Messiah* at Christmas, and I also enjoyed conducting the Christmas carol concerts, usually three of them, the first on Saturday night, repeated on Sunday afternoon and night. Gerry Temple, the orchestral manager, was an organist in a local church. He decided to form a choir made up of members of the orchestra, to sing in a service of Lessons and Carols in a beautiful little church in a village in Cheshire, just west of Manchester. Being good readers of music, the repertoire was quickly put together, and if I was up in Manchester for the Christmas concerts, I would join them. For untrained voices, the results were surprisingly good, and the whole ethos of Christmas was established for me listening to Margaret, one of the second violinists, proceeding from the rear of the church and singing, unaccompanied, the first verse of 'Once in Royal David's City'. It was exquisite, and very emotional. We all concentrated very hard, as we had no conductor, just Gerry on the organ, and even the impish Jimmy Murray added tone and lustre with his tenor voice. Organs, of course, can be temperamental at times, and on one occasion we all had to bite our lips very hard not to collapse in hysterics. Gerry got his feet tangled in the pedals, and the instrument obviously took great umbrage at this treatment, resulting in the most awful noise. The humour of the Halle players was legendary, and through this cacophony, inspired by Gerry Temple's previous existence in the Navy, one of the horn players, singing in the tenor section, yelled out, 'abandon ship!'

The opportunities afforded me by the Halle to develop and extend my choral repertoire were boundless. *Belshazzar's Feast*, of course, is a shining example, the television performance being the first time I'd ever conducted the work, which eventually over the years became our party piece. I added Elgar's *Dream of Gerontius*, and *The Kingdom* to my repertoire, along with Britten's *Spring Symphony* and his *War Requiem*, with soloists of the calibre of Robert Tear and Benjamin Luxon interpreting the moving war poems of Wilfred Owen, which Britten had so skilfully interwoven with the Latin text of the Requiem Mass. Vaughan Williams's *Sea Symphony* was added to my British repertoire and *Alexander Nevsky*, by Prokofiev, was again a work outside the normal sphere, as was Coleridge-Taylor's *Hiawatha*. Orff's *Carmina Burana* was beginning to become an audience favourite and I was now getting the scope and freedom to develop my maturing understanding and interpretation of the choral work most associated with me, Verdi's Requiem. The choir was an integral part of my unbroken, twenty-eight year period with the Hallé, and on the silver anniversary of my first conducting them I was presented with a silver baton on a wooden mount, inscribed with the words, 'From the Hallé Choir, presented with affection to Owain Arwel Hughes to celebrate our association of twenty-five years'.

Choral projects were to feature greatly in different degrees throughout my career. The Bournemouth Symphony Chorus was developing a sound reputation, and apart from the standard choral works I had much satisfaction giving a public performance of David Fanshawe's, *African Sanctus* which I'd recorded years earlier. Although I conducted all the assembled forces an engineer was needed to manipulate the sound equipment because of the way David had recorded the songs and dances of the different tribes he had encountered in Africa. Needless to say David took on that task, both of us revelling in the revival of our earlier collaboration and adapting an innovative, original concept for a stage performance. As a result of this connection with the Bournemouth Choir, I was invited to be conductor of the nearby Southampton Choral Society, charged with directing their performances during the season. I had a considerable regard for both these choruses, as they were heavily responsible for the survival and development of choral singing in that part of southern England, all their concerts much to their credit, accompanied by the Bournemouth Symphony Orchestra. It was a call from the Leicester Philharmonic Choir that was probably the most surprising, because of the work they had chosen to perform. Of all things, it was Berlioz's monumental conception of the Requiem Mass, with its imposing title, *Grande Messe des Morts*, Grand Mass of the Dead. I'll never forget the look on the face of the secretary of the choir, Tony Shilcock, when, on turning up to rehearse the choir, he asked me how many times I had conducted the work. Never, I replied. Actually, he shouldn't have been surprised, as performances of Berlioz's colossal undertaking were pretty rare – it required an enormous number of performers for Berlioz's demands to be even remotely feasible. It was essential that the orchestra should have quadruple woodwind, eight horns, eight trumpets and cornets, and a minimum of five sets of timps. Added to this, extra brass bands were to be placed in the four corners of the concert hall. The choir, naturally, had to be huge to contend with this battery of noise, and it's not surprising that it was nearly a century after the first performance that the work was heard again, because of the difficulty of assembling so many performers, and the astronomical costs. I shall always cherish this opportunity to study and perform such extraordinary music, leading to my being able to organise further performances, as a result of that initial experience. The Leicester Philharmonic Choir had an amazing will and capacity to programme unusual or demanding works. They organised a performance of my father's oratorio, *St David,* inviting the BBC Welsh Symphony Orchestra to accompany them. My father and mother were in the audience, delighted at the choir's committed and enthusiastic response.

Benjamin Britten's *War Requiem* was another challenge embarked upon by this enterprising body. As well as having a dynamic, visionary chairman in Tony Shilcock, they had an immensely supportive committee, with a secretary, Janet Simpson, who through her skills and charming personality, obtained the services of excellent singers. Having said that, many singers themselves spoke to me often of the stimulus to their careers as a result of these engagements. One evening, in a piano rehearsal for the forthcoming *War Requiem* performance, I was exhorting the men to respond to Britten's interpretation of the Latin words. The heavy rhythm of the basses in the 'Confutatis Maledictis', was answered by the quiet pleading 'Oro, supplex' of the tenors. Britten specifically indicates 'weeping' in his score, and in order to encourage the gentlemen, I said that they should all know everything about weeping, wailing and gnashing of teeth after the defeat of the England rugby team in Cardiff two days earlier. It was all good fun and they needed no further motivation.

At the end of the rehearsal, a rather attractive blonde lady approached me, wanting to take me up on my comments about the Wales/England match. She explained, with a mischievous grin, that her husband was Peter Wheeler, the Leicester forward who had played hooker for England in that match. He came to the concert, we had an amicable drink afterwards, and became firm friends. Two years later, he was again in Cardiff, with the same result, Wales being in one of their purple patches. We'd arranged for Peter and his wife Margaret to come for lunch to my parents' house on the Sunday. My mother and father were always excellent hosts, and welcomed the couple with their usual warm hospitality. The atmosphere was convivial, my father absolutely engrossed in listening to Peter's rugby stories, most of them unprintable, to the older man's wicked delight. On another occasion in our house in Harrow, Jean had looked after Peter and Margaret's two sons, Ben and Tom, so that Margaret could attend the England/Wales match at Twickenham and the post-match dinner. The next morning they arrived at our house accompanied by

Clive Woodward, later to become England's World Cup winning coach, and his wife Jane – Clive, a Leicester club partner of Peter's, having played centre for England in the same game. Paul Dodge, the other England centre in the international, and his wife Julia also joined us and a very happy Sunday lunch was enjoyed by all before their return to Leicester.

A Lions rugby tour was soon beckoning, and Peter suffered a disappointment when he was not selected, as he was obviously first choice for the position of hooker, his exclusion being undoubtedly political in order to accommodate a balance of players representing the four nations. I commiserated with Peter, but expressed my firm opinion that the tour was going to be a bad one and he would ultimately benefit from being well out of it. The tour turned out to be the disaster I'd predicted. The inevitable and logical result was that Peter was awarded the captaincy of England, a supreme honour. At about this time, strolling one night on Harrow on the Hill, I heard this voice shouting from across the road, 'Hello, I know you.' It transpired that the huge, shadowy figure was none other than Roger Uttley, an England rugby legend, who had recently taken up an appointment as head of sport at Harrow School. Here again, a friendship was formed, with both our families mixing easily.

Learning new repertoire always has been, and still is, an enterprise I find stimulating. Over the years, I have been in my element conducting first performances, particularly compositions I've commissioned myself, very aware of the responsibility towards the composer's intentions. Equally critical is the quality and merit of the performance, essential to the reputation of the composer and his critical acceptance. I have no doubt that having a father who was a composer must have influenced my attitude and sentiments. An incident in the National Eisteddfod that I had witnessed years earlier was typical of the frustrations and vulnerability of a composer. It was in Swansea in 1964, and the Eisteddfod choir was to premiere a newly commissioned work by my father entitled, *Pantycelyn*, which he would conduct. The libretto was compiled by Aneirin Talfan Davies, from a combination of the *Book of Common Prayer*, and the enormous wealth of hymns and lengthy poems which constituted the remarkable output of William Williams, from Pantycelyn. Aneirin Talfan Davies was the head of programmes for the BBC in Wales, concurrent with my father's BBC years, and this afforded a timely renewal of their earlier collaboration on *Dewi Sant*. A local choirmaster had been appointed by the Eisteddfod committee to train the choir, but at the same time, they organised a second concert which the chorus master would conduct. My father received a phone call from a singer who used to be a member of the BBC Welsh Chorus, an ensemble a little similar to today's BBC Chorus in London, entrusted with providing any musical items required for broadcasting, including the daily service. He voiced extreme concern that the chorus master was spending all the available time on his own concert, and very little on the new, far more difficult work. I drove my father to Swansea to appraise the situation, and it turned out, as anticipated, to be a complete and utter shambles. The evening culminated in a blazing row between my father and the chorus master in the car park. My father, somehow, managed to salvage some semblance of a performance out of the wreckage, thanks to the support of the BBC Welsh Orchestra. However, the lack of knowledge and technical training of the choir meant that the choristers couldn't sing both words and music together, resulting in La, La, La being substituted for the actual libretto. I learnt a sobering lesson in how irresponsible and selfish behaviour can be so futile and damaging.

I've already described earlier the gamble inherent in the formation of choirs for a one-off Eisteddfod. It's an excellent concept at its best, resulting in the continuance of the choir to the cultural advantage of that particular area. However it is so reliant not only on the standard and loyalty of the singers available, but also on the quality, enthusiasm and dedication of the chorus master. A National Eisteddfod in Cardiff always had the potential for something special, with its high-density population of working professionals and students in its colleges and universities. In Cardiff in 1960 my father and Mansel Thomas shared the choir training and conducting duties, their experience and professionalism integrating the choral forces into a formidable body to accomplish a prodigious feat in their execution of Beethoven's *Missa Solemnis*. Eighteen years later, the music committee was even more ambitious in its choice of music, and it was my privilege to hold the reins this time. The first half of the concert consisted solely of one work, Four Sacred Pieces. Verdi's last work begins and ends with a deeply profound, subtle interpretation of the evocative words of the Stabat Mater and Te Deum. To add to the difficulties and complexities for the Eisteddfod choir, Verdi places between these powerful orchestral and choral settings, two unaccompanied gems, the Ave Maria, and the beautiful Laudi alla Vergine Maria, for female voices. It is a work not often heard in this country, and the Eisteddfod choir dealt admirably with its intricacies. The second half presented a completely different series of musical and technical obstacles to overcome, Walton's *Belshazzar's Feast*. Stories still abound of the difficulties faced by the Leeds Festival Chorus in that first performance, and the problems encountered by the young Malcolm Sargent in persuading the sedate northerners, well versed in the traditional choral oratorios, to tackle the modernity of

Walton's exacting score, as well as its overtly pagan tone. Mercifully, Sargent was an excellent choral conductor and understood the psychology of handling large, choral forces. The Halle Choir's mastery of this work was the result of endless hours of patient work, and they often stressed to me the absolute necessity of learning Walton's music thoroughly and completely the very first time, as any bad habits were almost impossible to eradicate. It was most certainly a fascinating insight, I found, into a choral society's approach and strategy to a demanding, complex piece of music. Fair play to the Cardiff Eisteddfod Choir, they worked slavishly in their preparations, and as if the musicals demands placed before them were not daunting enough, their tough assignment was not made any easier by the fact that they had to sing Walton's brilliant realisation of Osbert Sitwell's libretto in a Welsh translation. I walked to the podium at the beginning of that second half to face a sea of white, terrified faces. My sister, who was singing in the soprano section, reminds me to this day that she stood there trembling, with her knees knocking together. I plunged into the opening brass fanfare and the dramatic male-voice opening prophecy, and with grit and determination, and inspired by the vivid orchestral effects, we safely arrived at the oratorio's thunderous conclusion.

My first association with a London choir was naturally a special occasion for me, and it was with the Royal Choral Society. I was well aware of the history of this famed society and I had often been in the audience as Sargent, their conductor for decades, weaved his magic, coaxing them to ever greater heights. Even their dress was distinctive, the ladies adorned in long, white, evening gowns. My debut with them took place in the Royal Albert Hall at their annual Good Friday performance of Handel's *Messiah*, which was always in the afternoon. It was an auspicious moment for me, and after, thankfully, a successful outcome, I felt it particularly odd for some reason that I should be leaving the Albert Hall in daylight after a concert. It was as if I needed the sanctuary of darkness to envelop me. By this time the choir had become more modern and adventurous in its outlook, and although rightly preserving the Good Friday tradition, it became much more enterprising, utilising highly trained, professional chorus masters. I experienced, and enjoyed the fruits of this development, conducting a performance with them for the BBC, of my father's *St David*.

I am extremely fortunate that I have been involved in all manner of choral enterprises, sometimes in the most unexpected of places. When Trinity College, Dublin, celebrated its four-hundredth anniversary, it was decided that the occasion had to be honoured with an unforgettable spectacle, ideally to involve as many contributors as possible. Mahler's Symphony of a Thousand seemed the perfect selection, described by Deryck Cooke, one of the world's outstanding Mahler scholars and specialists, as, 'the choral symphony of the twentieth century, as Beethoven's ninth was the choral symphony of the nineteenth. The RTE Symphony Orchestra and Concert Orchestra were combined, together with the extra brass bands, to form an instrumental gathering of well over 200 musicians. Added to these were ten choirs from Dublin and the surrounding neighbourhood, children's choirs, and eight soloists, easily surpassing the thousand performers preferably required for the ideal realisation of Mahler's epic vision, hence the sobriquet, 'The Symphony of a Thousand'. Just rehearsing the choral forces alone was a logistical nightmare, but despite the colossal numbers involved, I had many opportunities to engage with individuals and savour the warmth, generosity and hospitality of my Celtic cousins. We also had many amusing, if incredulous moments, when I teased them about how we had sent Patrick from Wales across the Irish Sea, to become their patron saint. Two performances took place on consecutive nights in the Point, a 6,000 seater, former dockside warehouse, adapted for large events. The first night was televised live, so that the whole country could participate in Trinity College's quarter centenary, celebrated in such an appropriate and magnificent style.

When my father retired from the BBC in 1971, he was invited to become music director of the Llangollen International Eisteddfod, a festival of singing and dancing, inaugurated in 1947 and open to competitors from all over the world. One of his first achievements was to create a world choir to perform Verdi's Requiem. It literally represented the world. Choir members consisted mainly of singers already in the town, competing with their respective choirs. Some though, had joined specifically for the opportunity to partake in a novel initiative, and enjoy Llangollen's unique ambience, and the harmony and concord created by such an eclectic collection of individuals. I trained the choir myself and it gave me much pleasure and satisfaction to unite the choristers of so many different nations, with their contrasting sounds and inflections. The universal appeal of Verdi's Requiem was the ideal vehicle to unify everyone, and was undoubtedly the inspiration for an especially moving, exhilarating, occasion. To everyone's surprise, and my personal pleasure, the choir gave an emotional, majestic rendition of the Welsh National Anthem, in four-part harmony, and perfect Welsh.

A further experience in Llangollen transpired to become quite a personal affair. Geraint, my son, was a member of his Junior School Choir in Harrow.

The music teacher, Joy Hill, was an enthusiast, with a remarkable talent for inspiring young children to express themselves through singing, and the multi-ethnic group she had formed, was a wonder to behold. Joy applied for, and was granted, the opportunity to compete at Llangollen. The appearance of this choir made up of a score of different races and colours would have warmed the hearts of those pioneering creators of Llangollen's original concept. The majority of Joy's choir would most likely never have left the environs of Harrow, let alone London, and would never before have seen cows and sheep in the countryside, and would have been stunned by the beauty and seren-ity of Llangollen, with the sparkling waters of the River Dee tumbling over the rocks. They acquitted themselves well in their allotted competition, and the highlight of the day was the amalgamation of all the youth choirs massed together on the Eisteddfod Field, singing together. I was granted the honour of conducting this extraordinary gathering, which was given added poignancy with three generations involved, my father the organiser, Geraint one of the singers, and myself.

ten
THE HUDDERSFIELD CHORAL

M Y FIRST CONTACT WITH the Huddersfield Choral Society was as a guest conductor in the late 1970s. Formed in 1836, the choir had a long-standing and deserved reputation as one of the finest in the United Kingdom. Totally amateur, the choir was able to tap into the rich vein of singers produced in the nonconformist, woollen mill tradition of West Yorkshire. Sir Malcolm Sargent, in tandem with his Royal Choral duties, had become its conductor in 1932. Since his death in 1967, no one had apparently followed in his footsteps and at the time I was engaged to conduct them, John Pritchard was nominally their conductor. However, his worldwide commitments made it difficult for him to visit Huddersfield often, hence my current invitation.

I arrived for the rehearsal of my first concert with the 'Choral' unannounced. As I quietly sat in the front row at Huddersfield Town Hall observing the bustling to and fro as the choristers arrived and greeted each other, I was approached by a gentleman who asked if I was the guest conductor. Although Herbert Bardgett had been its chorus master, he must have retired, because it was Douglas Robinson who welcomed me that evening, obviously guesting as a choirmaster. The work chosen by the committee for me to conduct was the full orchestral version of Rossini's *Petite Messe Solennelle*, a glorious sing for any choir, nothing solemn about it, and certainly at eighty-minutes long, full of rousing choruses, not at all petite.

The secretary of the choir was Richard Barraclough, with whom I built up a fine understanding, he being the model of professionalism, courtesy and organisation. After further engagements, he contacted me, detailing the wish of the officers and committee to consult with me and so a meeting was arranged in Manchester. It took place on a Saturday morning, I having conducted the Halle the night before, with another rehearsal and concert later that day. The committee had booked a room in the Midland Hotel, and when I arrived, I found a large group, sat in a semi circle, with one chair facing them. It was such an incongruous situation that I had the devil of a job not to burst into hysterical laughter, but at the same time, wondering where on earth all this presentation was leading. I was solemnly informed that for some time they felt that the standard and reputation of the choir had been deteriorating, and would I consider becoming the conductor of the choir, in much the same way Sir Malcolm Sargent had been previously. I was granted freedom to recommend a chorus master and given, quote 'carte blanche to bring the choir back to its former glory'. Although obviously surprised and flattered at the outcome of the meeting, the irony of the situation was not lost on me, the layout of the room arranged as if I was being interviewed for a job which I had applied for, rather than about to be offered me. Together with Richard Barraclough and a lifelong patron and benefactor of the society, Bill Drake, I set about making plans for the revival of the Society's fortunes.

My first recommendation was that we should start with a new, fresh chorus master and proposed Nina Walker, a first-rate repetiteur and assistant chorus master at the Royal Opera House, Covent Garden. If she could deal with the histrionics and temperamental behaviour of prima donnas, and manage the onerous schedule of an opera chorus, then training the Huddersfield Choral would hold no fears. We made a great team, she urging the choristers with tact and diplomacy, and playing the piano when I rehearsed the choir myself. I'd noticed early on that there was no real camaraderie and fellowship amongst the choir members. They would turn up for rehearsals, naturally becoming familiar with those near them in the choir, and then at the end, disappear into the night. I felt that a good team spirit was essential if we were to scale the heights, and so I suggested a workshop weekend away from home, where we could have quality rehearsal time, and bond together through social interaction.

It was a bit of a gamble, as nothing like it had ever occurred in the history of the 'Choral', as it was popularly called, but the committee set about organising the gathering with enthusiasm. The venue chosen was the Grand Hotel in Scarborough, North Yorkshire. Jean and I had visited Scarborough with Lisa when she was very young, and noticed what a pleasant, well-appointed hotel it was. When instructions for the weekend's arrangements arrived in the post one morning, reminding us not to forget to bring our soap and towels, we thought it was a joke and, believing it was someone's idea of a leg pull, ignored the advice. On the Friday of the workshop weekend, I had been working with the Halle Orchestra, and with Jean, Lisa and Geraint in tow, left Manchester by car on a dismal, wet evening. As we crossed eastwards over the Pennines, the weather became increasingly more atrocious, and by the time we approached Scarborough, we were greeted with icy sleet, blown by a full-blooded gale. Imagine our abject horror when we turned into the hotel square to be confronted with a garishly lit building with the words 'Welcome to Butlins' emblazoned in blue neon lights. We were shown up to our accommodation, all four of us in one large room facing the sea, to be greeted with the curtains flying at us, completely horizontal, blasted at us by what appeared to be a hurricane attacking off the North Sea. The first thing we had to do of course, was to go out and buy some soap and towels. As there was no food provided in the hotel, we sent out for fish and chips. The bonding exercise was beginning to work, as everyone found themselves in the same, unaccustomed, unfamiliar predicament. Humour was beginning to reveal itself, and one wag actually arranged for the fish and chips to be delivered on a silver platter.

Things got even more bizarre, as the next morning the stairs down to the dining room were lined with Butlins' Red Coats, greeting us with shouts of Hi de hi! We returned the gesture, with the 160 strong choir, in perfect, four-part harmony, treating the hotel staff to a rendition of 'Be present at our table Lord', sung to the stately tune Rimington, complete with a firm, rousing final Amen to conclude, a pre-meal grace the like of which none of us or them had ever heard before. Rehearsals proved to be of inestimable value, with Nina a massive support on the piano, as we pushed the choristers ever harder to achieve our ultimate goal of an outstanding choir. The quality of voices was undoubtedly there, the challenge being to harness that tone, allied with a thorough knowledge of the music, strict discipline in dynamics, accuracy and seamless, musical phrasing. As it turned out, the hilarity and incredulity of the circumstances we found ourselves in proved to be the perfect, though unforeseen catalyst, that threw everyone together, releasing them from their earlier shyness and reserve. The result was an unprecedented breakthrough in all respects, and the choir returned to Huddersfield full of esprit de corps and confidence.

The tradition at the Huddersfield Choral Society was to appoint a president for a two-year period, sometimes serving the previous two as vice-president. These presidents were usually local businessmen for which the presidency was an honour and a privilege, as well as an opportunity to financially support the society. It was at Scarborough that Jean, Lisa, Geraint and I began our special friendship with George and Nancy Slater that still flourishes today. George was a baritone with thirty years' loyal service to the Society, and was just beginning his two-year tenure as vice president, before assuming the presidency. He was an extremely popular choice, especially because of the rarity of it being allocated to a choir member. I cannot understate how important and vital George's contribution was to my success at Huddersfield.

The new quality of the choir was now attracting attention. Tickets for the 'Choral's' season of concerts were often passed down from generation to generation, including an annual *Messiah*. This was then repeated, open to the general public. Soon the demand for the public performance tickets was at a premium, with people queuing overnight outside the Town Hall to get the chance to hear the choir live. I now felt the choir was ready to expand its horizons, and in January 1982, the choir paid its first visit to London's Royal Festival Hall. We presented Elgar's *Dream of Gerontius* to a critical, discerning London audience, and all the hard work was justified when we were rewarded with a standing ovation from the capacity audience. No less a critic than the legendary William Mann wrote in *The Times*, 'Praise to the holiest, its last pages projected by Mr Hughes with a tingling instancy and almost no application of breaks at the final cadence that made me long to rise from my seat and cheer'.

Meanwhile, Arthur Owen, whom I had met years earlier in my student days collecting the conducting prize from Ricordi, had been my manager for some time. He and Jean travelled together by train on the Friday of a Huddersfield Choral concert, and as soon as the train had left King's Cross Station Arthur would disappear, returning armed with two pork pies and a bottle of red wine. His partner of thirty-one years, George, had died, and managing me was the perfect antidote to his grief. He always regarded me as the son he could never have, and together with Jean, Lisa and Geraint, we forged a link that is still unbroken today. He had become closely acquainted with Sueann and Denny, South Africans, and the granddaughters of T. B. Davis, who made his fortune as a shipping magnate, passing on his considerable wealth to the two sisters.

When the Puccini copyright expired in 1974, Ricordi Milan, the headquarters, panicked and closed all the management offices, including London. Arthur was given a golden handshake and, together with Sueann, formed an artists' agency, Owen Evans. At first, they dealt mainly with singers. During his career at Ricordi, Arthur had worked a great deal with singers, supporting and encouraging them in the development of their careers. Through his many years working for Ricordi, he had close ties with the Royal Opera House, so that his inside knowledge of the needs of both singers and opera houses served him well in the formative years of the agency. I eventually came under the Owen Evans management, Arthur becoming my personal manager, guiding my developing career with care, understanding and wise judgement.

It was through this connection with Sueann that I came into contact with her sister Denny Dayviss, a colourful character, a bit of a maverick, the complete antithesis to the businesslike Sueann. Denny had made quite a name for herself promoting a string of concert performances of opera in the Royal Festival Hall, being the first to introduce such names as Montserrat Caballé, Plácido Domingo and a very young José Carreras to London. Her first amazing venture, probably highly risky at the time, was a production of Meyerbeer's *Les Huguenots* at the Royal Albert Hall in November, 1968. It was the first introduction to London of a soprano who was later to achieve stratospheric status, Joan Sutherland. She was joined by another singer who was also to achieve worldwide stardom, Martina Arroyo, the whole proceedings conducted by Joan Sutherland's future husband, Richard Bonynge.

She decided to resurrect her scheme, declaring adamantly, as was her wont, that she wanted me to conduct, and asked which opera I wished it to be. I replied, without any hesitation, Puccini's *Turandot*. At dinner that night, I explained to Denny, with Arthur also present, that in the back of my mind, I vaguely remembered in an article, Puccini describing how he had written a duet in the same vein as in Wagner's *Tristan and Isolde*. Along with this, I had long felt the shape of the last movement to be truncated, and the final climax too abrupt. Then I had one of my prophetic moments.

When I was a student at Cardiff University, I used to accompany, on the piano, a theological student who, although entering the ministry, used to sing in competitions and social gatherings, blessed as he was with a beautiful tenor voice. I used a copy of *Turandot* I'd found amongst my father's music, which only had the accompaniment, but no vocal lines. I sped home as fast as I could, and sure enough, there, towards the end of the final act, was all this extra music, which didn't make much sense without any vocals, but definitely deserved further exploration. I was still in contact with Ricordi, as they had a library in the UK, in a country mansion in the picturesque little village of Chesham in Buckinghamshire, northwest of London. David Halliday, who was in charge of the library, worked wonders, thanks to his intimate knowledge of the machinations of Italians, and I was granted permission to visit the main Ricordi library in Milan. On the evening flight to Italy I was sitting quietly in the front-row window seat when a lady rushed in at the very last

minute, and sat down in the seat next to me. After apologising profusely for
her intrusion, she breathlessly explained that she had just dashed from recording sessions with a singer called Elton John. I must confess I'd never heard of
this fellow at the time, but my female companion was excitedly clutching a
batch of tapes that she considered priceless.

The next morning I made my way out to the Ricordi archives in a suburb
of Milan, to come face to face with obfuscation and delaying tactics. I stood
my ground, annoyed and frustrated at such behaviour, pointing out that I
had permission from the highest authority to see everything in the *Turandot*
archives. Ultimately, common sense prevailed, and the relevant documenta-
tion brought up from the vaults. If my female companion on the plane had
been excited with her recording tapes, it paled into insignificance at my reaction to my discovery. There, casually enfolded in a brown paper bag, was
the full score, in pencil, of the orginal ending by Alfano, Puccini having died
before its completion. The Alfano ending which has always been performed,
and is still in universal use today, is quite short, but the version I had discovered
contained the fabled duet and some additional choruses, leading naturally to a
noble climax. After the final chord the score is signed, 'Fine. Franco Alfano,
28 January, 1926'. To add intriguing substance to my discovery I found,
among the documents, pieces of manuscript detailing how Puccini himself had
intended completing his opera. I took my newly found treasure back to the
centre of Milan, to the head office of Ricordi, and obtained a meeting with the
director of the company. I requested permission to perform this new-found
version in London, as Denny had assured me that if I did find something, she
would include it in her planned *Turandot* concert performance. The Ricordi
director assured me that she personally would supervise the copying of the
score on to a micro film and send it to London so that David Halliday and his
team could prepare a full score and vocal, choral and orchestral parts.

The performance took place in the Barbican Concert Hall in February,
1982. Denny had engaged the London Symphony Orchestra, soprano Silvia
Sass, tenor Franco Bonisolli, and the mezzo-soprano Barbara Hendricks. The
chorus, of course, had to be the Huddersfield Choral, whose blazing sound
rounded off the whole, unique evening. Bonisolli had quite a reputation for
his capricious temperament, although I had already had effective, problem-free
piano rehearsals with both him and Silvia Sass. He had been bemoaning the air
conditioning at the Barbican, and the way it would badly harm his vocal cords
and singing quality. So on the first morning's rehearsal, with the air conditioning switched off, and the orchestra sweating profusely and in much discomfort,

Bonisolli left the stage still grumbling and complaining. I'd had quite enough of this childish, unnecessary posturing, and called his bluff by ignoring him and carrying on with the orchestra. Their playing was, of course, ravishing, and it demonstrated how Puccini's incomparable melodies, harmonies and subtleties, were all represented in the orchestra. Bonisolli soon crept back up onto the stage, realising that he was not totally indispensable, and reverted to the tenor I had known earlier in private. In the performance, his singing was top class, executing the numerous top Cs in this extended version with consummate ease. However he just could not resist the temptation, even in a concert performance, of grasping any opportunity to upstage his fellow soloists, much to their annoyance. Denny's brave, daring production was some accomplishment and I was able to promote her entrepreneurial skills by appearing that evening, live on Channel 4's first news programme, television's latest station having been inaugurated that day.

Following the choir's achievement in the Royal Festival Hall, further visits were arranged, including a performance of *Carmina Burana*. The *Messiah* had become synonymous with Huddersfield again, and it seemed the obvious work to attract a capacity audience to the Royal Festival Hall to support the work of NCH, the National Children's Home (now known as Action for Children), a charity of which I had become vice president. My daughter, Lisa, presented Diana, Princess of Wales, with a bouquet at a pre-concert reception. After the concert, I conversed amicably with her and the Prince of Wales, enjoying their observations of the concert, as well as exchanging well-informed views of their tastes in music. I had first met Princess Diana in a piano competition I had conducted, in her presence in Newport, South Wales. While the adjudicators were deliberating, we had the opportunity to relax and chat at ease, in complete agreement as to who should be the winner. Her reaction and disbelief at the choice of winner was a source of amusement to both of us, something she reminded me of frequently.

The growing reputation of the Huddersfield *Messiah* had a very unexpected reaction in, of all places, Wales. Alun Hoddinott had for some years been running a very imaginative and successful Festival of Contemporary Music in Cardiff. He was intrigued, and as a first class musician, certainly very pleased and appreciative of the high standard of the Huddersfield Choir which was being widely written and talked about. He proposed that we perform the *Messiah* at his Festival. The orchestra were all players from the BBC Welsh, engaged out of contract, on a freelance basis, called in the business, 'up the line'. After singing a chorus or two, I stepped off the rostrum and quietly said to the players that the choir was taking them to the cleaners. They all ruefully agreed, saying that they were so used to choirs singing behind the beat. They quickly realised that they were accompanying a choir that not only sang on the beat, but were crisp and incisive. For a change, it was the orchestra that had to adjust. They absolutely loved it, and responded magnificently.

In meetings with Simon Foster, a recording executive at EMI, I discussed how we could utilise the enormous potential of the Huddersfield choir. Its superb quality and firmly established reputation was a vindication of the trust placed in me by the committee, and their acceptance of my choice of chorus master, the first female in the choir's long history. Simon proposed we embark on a project to record a disc of hymns, combining the Huddersfield sound with its nonconformist, hymn-singing heritage, similar to that of Wales. We recorded the album over three nights in the spacious acoustics of an empty Huddersfield Town Hall, the public response even surprising the all-knowing, practised eye of Simon. It attained gold in its sales, an amazing achievement for a classical album, and the actual gold disc has the iconic HMV label of the dog poking its nose into the open end of the phonograph, as if listening to his master's voice emanating from the machine, the last disc to have this symbol on its label. This outstanding success was followed up with a further album, this time of Christmas carols. The success was repeated, and a further gold disc awarded.

Nina Walker, who had established such a rapport with the choristers and done sterling work, now found herself faced with a dilemma. There were problems at the Royal Opera House, and she had to give more time as a repetiteur to the soloists. She also had to assume full time, direct responsibility for the chorus. It became abundantly clear that her health was now suffering as a result of this punishing schedule. She became aware that the resultant tiredness and fatigue was making her fractious and irascible, naturally upsetting the choristers, so she reluctantly relinquished her post at Huddersfield. A recently retired chorister from the King's Singers asked if he could have a few rehearsal sessions with the choir. In his charming manner and easy, friendly attitude, he appealed to the choir, and was appointed chorus master.

When I was appointed conductor of the 'Choral' in 1980, I was aware of their 150th anniversary in six years time, hence my approach to Walton, with its sad conclusion. It was now time to commission, and I approached Paul Patterson, professor of composition at the Royal Academy of Music, who already had an impressive reputation and a substantial catalogue of publications. I was well acquainted with his music and style, having recorded an album of his orchestral works for EMI with the London Philharmonic

Orchestra. We discussed my earlier invitation for Walton to set the Stabat Mater, and he readily agreed to compose a choral work on the same text. As the anniversary year approached, I had already had to have a few very private words with the chorus master. I had noticed that the standard of preparation of the choir was slipping, and he was beginning to usurp his role as chorus master, getting very involved on his weekly visits with the planning and organisation.

My experience over many years of dealing with composers was that it was disastrous if they were present at early rehearsals of their compositions, as performers struggled to get to grips with the new music. I'd discovered it was psychologically unwise even with a professional orchestra, but with an amateur choir, however good, time and patience is needed. I'd seen this proved, time and time again. Although I'd warned the chorus master of the inherent dangers of this early exposure, he took it upon himself, against my express wishes, to invite Paul up to Huddersfield for an early rehearsal. I knew nothing of this until it was time for me to rehearse the choir myself, and discovered that Paul, although I had not been informed, had made changes due to his inevitable panic caused by listening to the unprepared choir. Its world premiere eventually took place without the unnecessary changes, and restored to its original, to Paul's immense satisfaction.

Following the success of previous Festival Hall appearances, a performance of *Carmina Burana* had been arranged. The concert, as with all previous Royal Festival Hall concerts, was on a Saturday, and I would always do the final rehearsal with an already well-prepared choir, not on the night before, but one week earlier. This meant that those wishing to spend a weekend in London could do so, and those coming by coach on the day were ready for a very early start. I went up to Huddersfield to find the standard of the choir totally unsatisfactory. After the quality of the choir in a performance of the same work only three years earlier at the Festival Hall, I was naturally a little perturbed, and asked a general, rhetorical question, 'what am I supposed to do with this?' I was looking around at the choir, and the question was aimed at no one in particular so I was a little surprised and disappointed that the chorus master took the comment personally and complained bitterly to the committee. He had, without any consultation, arranged that he would take an all-day rehearsal the next day. A little late, I ruefully observed. The day at the Royal Festival Hall was a most unpleasant experience, but on the podium, free from encumbrances, I enjoyed the brilliance of the Royal Philharmonic Orchestra in Mussorgsky's orchestral showpiece, *Pictures at an Exhibition*, and with their sturdy support, steered the choir through *Carmina Burana*. The ensuing aftermath was that I requested the chorus master's annual contract should not be renewed. Sometime later I had a phone call saying, that although I was considered 'the best choral conductor they'd every experienced', they could not acquiesce to my request.

In the summer of 1986, my father had been commissioned to write a choral work, which he entitled *Gloria Patri*, to celebrate the fortieth anniversary of the Llangollen International Eisteddfod. With the help of that august secretary, Richard Barraclough, who first invited me to conduct the choir, I arranged that the 'Choral' would perform at this very personal occasion, along with the Halle Orchestra. I rehearsed the choir myself; they learnt the music quickly and easily, resulting in a very satisfying outcome. It was to be my last concert with the Huddersfield Choral Society. Having thought long and hard about my position, I concluded it was untenable, and tendered my resignation. One of my main regrets was that Richard Barraclough, a singing member of the choir, was about to begin his stint as President. I would have relished the prospect of our collaboration. The Christmas carol recording described earlier, like the previous Hymns album, was recorded over three nights. At the end of the third night, with the recording successfully completed, I announced to a stunned choir that as a recommendation I had made on purely artistic grounds had been refused, I therefore had no option but to resign.

Above: *With Jean, Lisa and Geraint, in the conductor's room at the Royal Albert Hall.*

Right: *At EMI receiving the last gold disc to carry the original HMV label, next to the painting 'His Master's Voice' by Francis Barraud ARA.*

Above: *With HRH
The Prince of Wales at
Highgrove, in 1990.*

Left: *With HRH The
Queen Mother at the
opening of St David's
Hall, Cardiff, in 1983.*

Rehearsing for the Welsh Proms with Max Boyce, Nerys Hughes, Neil Kinnock and Cliff Morgan, in 1987.

With Jean, Lisa and Geraint, after receiving a University of Wales doctorate at Bangor University, in 1991.

Conducting Shirley Bassey at Cardiff Arms Park with the Royal Philharmonic Orchestra and a male choir of 10,000, in 1994.

Left: *With Jean supporting my leg in plaster, following the Pavarotti incident, in 1996.*

Below: *Receiving the OBE from Her Majesty The Queen at Buckingham Palace, in 2004.*

Owain Arwel Hughes OBE.

With Jean at the unveiling on Shrewsbury station platform in 2004 of a plaque commemorating the composing of 'Tydi a Roddaist'.

With Geraint, Jean and Lisa at Buckingham Palace, after being awarded the CBE, in 2010.

With Jean and our granddaughters, Clementine and Elektra, in 2012.

eleven
THE WELSH PROMS

S A YOUNGSTER GROWING UP IN CARDIFF, I was well aware of the frequent demands for a concert hall. The City Hall, with its impressive staircase and marble statues, was the only building capable of accommodating an orchestra, but with its tricky reverberations, long, narrow shape and limited capacity, it wasn't really adequate for public performance. Then one day, out of the blue, came the surprise announcement that a brand-new, purpose-built concert hall was to be erected, its construction to commence immediately. Harlech Television, Wales's independent television company, was producing a documentary, chronicling the development of the building, and asked if I would spend some time in the shell of the hall and assess its potential. I made my first observation before I'd even entered the hall. The location couldn't have been more perfect, right in the very heart of the city. Although still being built its configuration was already taking shape. The positioning of the stage, encircled by different levels of tiered seating, was clearly visible, with excellent sightlines from all angles. There was certainly no concert hall of this design anywhere in the United Kingdom. Standing there, gazing at this amazing structure, I had another of my prophetic moments. I knew, with absolute certainty, that my future destiny was bound up with this concert hall. It was certainly not a flight of fancy, but total conviction.

St David's Hall was officially opened by Queen Elizabeth, the Queen Mother, on 15 February, 1983. It was followed by a concert given by the BBC Welsh Symphony Orchestra, as it was then called. I certainly didn't know when I was given the distinction of conducting this festive gala, what it would lead to. The hall turned out to be exceptional, beyond everyone's wildest dreams, recognised by all visiting musicians from far and wide as easily the best in the United Kingdom and amongst the finest in Europe. It was this unique, distinctive concert hall, alongside my familiarity with the impact of the Halle Proms that inspired me to create the Welsh Proms. I presented my concept to the chairman of Cardiff City Council, Ron Watkiss, a Conservative councillor, and together we obtained unanimous, all-party support for the project. St David's Hall is owned and administered by the council and this uniform consensus was a vitally important boost before launching the project.

The opening concert of the very first Welsh Proms took place in July, 1986. I sat in my dressing room and, probably for the first time in my career, wondered if there would be any sort of an audience at all. There had been plenty of cynical mutterings leading up to these pioneering inaugural proms, with gloomy, pessimistic, doom-laden predictions. I walked out to rapturous applause from a capacity audience and without any further ado, facing the ever-faithful, Halle Orchestra, I signalled the opening trumpet motif of Mussorgsky's *Pictures at an Exhibition* in Ravel's dazzling orchestration. It was the best possible opening night, and the triumphant evening was rounded off with the catchy, syncopated rhythms of *Carmina Burana*, the Halle Choir adding vibrancy and fervour to the crackling atmosphere. As I'd already discovered with the Halle Proms, the Last Night is a guaranteed sell-out, so I came up with the idea of designating a charity for this closing concert. In the traditional speech, I talked about the unselfish dedication and often lifesaving activities of the chosen charity, and encouraged the audience to contribute generously to the collection. Over the years, a considerable amount has been collected for a variety of good causes, and we are still the only Proms to do this.

To everyone's relief, the first-ever Welsh Proms went without a hitch, and we were able to establish, even from the start, our own style of Last Night, the audience participation and singing being especially fresh and distinctive. I was unable to use the BBC Welsh Symphony Orchestra, but I engaged the players on a freelance basis, calling it simply the Welsh Symphony Orchestra. They responded very well to the unpredictable nature of a last night prom, and it was particularly heart-warming for me that these players whom I knew so well, should be involved in this ground-breaking adventure.

Two days later, on a Monday morning, Arthur Owen had arranged that I should meet John Drummond, the controller of Radio Three and supremo of the London Proms. I was ushered up to his office to find him standing in the middle of the room waving a copy of that morning's *Times*, pointing out a photograph of the Last Night of the inaugural Welsh Proms. He proceeded to poke fun at me and the whole concept, taking great delight in ridiculing such a pointless, absurd fantasy. I stood there, facing this cynical outburst, slightly mystified that probably the most powerful, influential music administrator in the land, and director of the Proms, established nearly 100 years earlier by the genius of Sir Henry Wood, should find it necessary to be so scornful. I left, knowing full well that there were some perilous waters ahead of me.

I originally set up the Welsh Proms to utilise the incomparable qualities and attractions of St David's Hall, as well as filling the void caused by the dearth of activities in the summer in Cardiff. Another aspect of the concept was to encourage people to use Cardiff as a tourist centre, with so many exquisite haunts to explore. The Vale of Glamorgan, the Gower, the Brecon Beacons, the castles, museums and countryside walks are all within easy reach, and the position of the hall in the city centre is a perfect focal point for friends to gather and socialise. Programmes were designed to accommodate all tastes in music, enticing people who had never before experienced live music-making to take the plunge, hopefully lured also by the warm vibes circulating regarding the amiable, welcoming atmosphere. A special concert was instigated immediately in the first year, designed specifically to attract families. Narrative pieces such as, *Peter and the Wolf*, *Tubby the Tuba*, *Paddington Bear* and *The Snowman* were presented, with stars of radio and television illuminating the plots in their distinctive manner. One very unusual work caused such hilarity one year that everyone, including the orchestra, collapsed in fits of laughter. I had programmed wisely, or maybe to my folly, I am not quite sure which to this day, Malcolm Arnold's quirky, witty *Grand, Grand Overture*, featuring vacuum cleaners, and all sorts of sundry household apparatus. Manipulating these exotic instruments were well-known celebrities of the time, including Neil and Glenys Kinnock, the Emanuels, who had designed Princess Diana's wedding dress, Doug Mountjoy, champion snooker player of his day, Nerys Hughes, Max Boyce and Cliff Morgan.

However, the principal purpose of the Welsh Proms was to present a subtle mixture of mainstream and unfamiliar repertoire, performed by a blend of high-quality soloists and the finest orchestras. One of my prime intentions from the very beginning was to have a firm policy of commissioning new works by Welsh composers. My first assignment was to discuss with Alun Hoddinott, the senior Welsh composer, the particular scheme I had in mind. I was keen on a virtuoso orchestral piece, as I was Associate Conductor of the Philharmonia Orchestra at the time, and so we came up with the idea of what would eventually be his Concerto for Orchestra. We agreed that it would not be handed over at the last minute, but in plenty of time for the orchestra parts to be well prepared, the players, particularly the percussion, to be organised, and with adequate time for rehearsal. Alun delivered the commissioned opus as promised, producing one of his finest works, a stiff examination for the players which they welcomed, and which was well received by the audience. Having laid out my commissioning policy, this was quite some bench mark for future composers to follow, resulting in nearly a score of excellent compositions from such composers as William Mathias, Karl Jenkins and Gareth Wood. I also appreciated very much the endorsement of this strategy by the hall's management, and the financial help from the Welsh Arts Council.

After the success of the first year, I set about seeking sponsorship. Midland Bank came up with a novel idea of financing young people to attend rehearsals during the Proms, which gave me the opportunity to interact with them, discussing what they were seeing and hearing – very revealing, and never was the saying 'out of the mouths of babes and sucklings' so true. This was organised in conjunction with an essay competition, another creative challenge for the children. Lloyds Bank were also regular sponsors over a period of seventeen years, and the philanthropy of Welsh Brewers afforded me the luxury of programming works never before heard in Wales. Mahler's 'Symphony of a Thousand', Prokofiev's oratorio, *Alexander Nevsky*, Richard Strauss's mammoth *Alpine Symphony* were ambitious Welsh premieres. We reflected contemporary scholarship in the first hearing in Wales of Anthony Payne's elaboration of Elgar's sketches for a symphony into a complete symphonic form, thus providing an intrigued musical world with Elgar's third symphony.

Perhaps one of the most unusual and remarkable achievements was the first and only presentation in Wales of Sibelius's youthful, *Kullervo* symphony. Only recently resurrected, it's written for a large symphony orchestra with a major role for a male voice choir. There had been a few performances in England, but always with a Finnish conductor and a male choir imported from Finland, as the text was in Finnish. The Treorchy Male Choir, under its conductor at the time, John Jenkins, accepted the challenge and sang the music from memory. I wanted the performance in the original language. Fortunately the wife of one of the directors of Welsh Brewers was Finnish, so she coached the men of the Rhondda and the two Welsh soloists, Helen Field and Jason Howard, so that we could give the first performance of this work ever by non-Finnish singers.

It's been the tradition in the Henry Wood Proms in London to play Wood's *Fantasia on Sea Songs* to close the Last Night. For the first few years, we ended the Welsh Proms in exactly the same way. Once the Welsh Proms were well established, I asked the Welsh composer, Gareth Wood if he could compose a similar Fantasia but incorporating traditional Welsh tunes, folk songs, and hymns. We now have our own, unique way of concluding the Welsh Proms, audience participation being a vital feature of the proceedings, especially the stirring singing of popular hymns in both English and Welsh.

After a concert sponsored by the Welsh Brewers, they used to hold a reception in the hospitality room in their brewery. I particularly enjoyed the party after the Last Night, my first opportunity to really relax after quite a gruelling round of rehearsals, concerts, television, radio and newspaper interviews. It was always a relief to see ideas formulated a year or more earlier come to fruition. I never took any success for granted, enjoying that year's particular achievement but knowing full well that the public's expectation, quite rightly, becomes ever higher. The Welsh Brewers' hospitality was second to none, with birthdays and anniversaries always celebrated with suitable mementos. One year, I was especially honoured to be presented with a 'Grog', a miniature statue, the subject caricatured as a rugby player. In my case, I was kitted out in a Welsh international jersey and white shorts, with a rugby ball in my left hand, a baton in my right, and a treble clef where the number would be on the back of the shirt.

In 1991, Clive Smart was retiring after thirty-three years as general manager of the Halle Concerts Society. The Halle Orchestra played in the Last Night that year, and some members of the orchestra were invited to the brewery to provide some entertainment. Clive was presented with an engraved silver tankard, and he still talks proudly and affectionately about the special way his retirement was celebrated.

Over the years, now totalling twenty-seven, our output has consisted of a vast array of choral and orchestral gems, classical, romantic and contemporary. Apart from the various masses, requiems and oratorios, our audience has enjoyed acts from *La Bohème* and *Madame Butterfly*, a complete concert performance of Verdi's *Nabucco* and an unforgettable semi-staged presentation of Puccini's tragic opera, *Tosca*, with a magnificent portrayal of the villainous Scarpia by Bryn Terfel. By now, generations upon generations have experienced the Welsh Proms, and been introduced to the rich, inexhaustible store of music. The shape and facilities at St David's Hall meant we could have a promenade area right up to the front of the stage. It provided a close, personal contact with the promenaders, and I shall never forget one night feeling a tug at my trouser leg, and a little girl handing me a sweet. This reflected perfectly for me the warm, cosy, safe atmosphere that had been created, and I doubt if we'll ever know the true extent of the Welsh Proms' influence.

I had for some considerable time been aware of the gulf between the final student years of an instrumentalist, and the harsh reality of life as a professional musician. Youth and student orchestras provided opportunities for playing together, but these were far removed from the relentless, everyday demands of earning a living, let alone the rigid self-discipline and preparation for auditions needed even to obtain work in the first place. There was now the opportunity, with the facilities available in St David's Hall and the stability and well-established nature of the Welsh Proms, to do something about the situation, to fill the gap, between college and the profession. Advertisements were sent out describing the precise constitution of a special orchestra with an experienced orchestral manager to oversee its running. For me, this was extremely important, as I was adamant that the young players should be exposed to the everyday conditions of a professional orchestra, incorporating the normal three-hour rehearsal times with the precise breaks as set out by the Musicians' Union. Punctuality, preparation, concert dress code, these are the regular disciplines and expectations, and this specially formed orchestra was subjected to the same rigours, and accountable for any lapses. Concerto accompaniment is a standard requirement, and so we engaged the Norwegian violinist, Arve Tellefsen, in order for the players to learn how to listen carefully and respond meticulously to the demands of a soloist of international repute. The result was everything I'd hoped for, the determination, resolution and commitment truly inspirational. The following year, S4C decided to participate in the venture. As well as providing coverage of an event in the Welsh Proms, it was a sure-fire vehicle to display the talents of Welsh youth to the whole country and beyond. I was determined that the youngsters should have an insight into every facet of public scrutiny and learn to concentrate deeply, shutting out all the kinds of distractions and interruptions that they would inevitably face. Television has all sorts of peculiar demands – obtrusive, sometimes blinding lighting, cameras moving backwards and forwards on a dolly on railway tracks, and probably the most disconcerting of all, a camera right in your face, showing close up how the instrument is played, and the effects achieved. It's a modern-day demand, another requirement and discipline I was anxious the players should experience.

In many ways, this decade, the 1980s, seemed to combine for me consolidation and further development. Radio Two continued to seek my services, much to my satisfaction, as their various producers were always coming up with bright new ideas which I found very stimulating. The relationship with the BBC Concert Orchestra was expanding, with recordings such as Walton's *Te Deum* and his rarely heard *Gloria*, broadcast in conjunction with London's full-time professional choral ensemble, the BBC Chorus. Gounod's *Messe Solennelle de Sainte Cécile* was again an example of the highly unusual programme suggestions which this radio channel encouraged, along with a broadcast of my father's *St David*, the BBC Concert Orchestra combining this time with the Royal Choral Society. Through the connection with Radio Two, I was able to obtain the services of the BBC Concert Orchestra for an appearance at the Welsh Proms, which resulted in an unexpected bonus. The programme opened with the *Carnival Overture* by Dvořák, Barry Tuckwell was the soloist in Mozart's fourth horn concerto, and the second half consisted of one work, the first symphony by Sibelius. This is where my regular work with the Halle Orchestra was really beginning to pay dividends, as not only was my own repertoire increasing, but I was having the opportunity, through repeated performances, of expanding and broadening my understanding, conception and interpretation of these masterworks. I was later led to understand that the Radio Two producer had a battle royal with Radio Three's controller John Drummond, who protested vehemently that the concert should not be broadcast at all lest it compete with his London Proms. The rendition by the BBC Concert Orchestra was admirable, and the happy outcome was that a CD was produced from the broadcast tape to accompany the first-ever edition of the *BBC Music Magazine*.

During this period, I was appointed associate conductor of two very different orchestras, the BBC Welsh Symphony, and the Philharmonia in London. As Head of Music, BBC Wales, until 1971, my father had decided that I should have no connection with the Welsh orchestra. He was well aware of the prevalence of nepotism, and was ultra-sensitive to being accused of even a hint of it, let alone being charged with it. It was a firm, if harsh stand to take, one I respected, and I likewise couldn't have lived, let alone performed, under such an accusation or allegation. My father's successor, granted two years in the post to enhance his pension, didn't have the slightest interest in me, branding me contemptuously as some sort of light music conductor. My agent at the time was Basil Horsfield, whose main artist was John Pritchard, and who had dealings also with Geraint Evans in opera. Basil approached the BBC music department in Cardiff, enquiring about an engagement for me in the normal manner, to receive the reply from one of the producers, 'I had already had a fair crack of the whip with them'. This seemed a rather peculiar response, as I had never, ever, conducted the orchestra, nor had there been any previous advances.

So it was a pleasant surprise when one day I was contacted personally by Arnold Lewis. Many years earlier Mansel Thomas, conducting a studio production of Menotti's *Amahl and the Night Visitors*, had requested some extra singers to augment the small chorus used for the daily service. I had sung in the Cardiff Eisteddfod Choir for the Proclamation Concert in 1959 conducted by my father and Mansel Thomas, who had noticed me in the choir and asked my father would I like to join the chorus for the studio recording. Arnold was the producer, and I found him very musical, instructive, and with an easy, relaxed studio manner. After taking time to settle into his new appointment as Head of Music, Arnold became aware of the fact I'd never appeared before the orchestra, advising me of his wish to rectify the situation. He organised a studio performance of Beethoven's third symphony the *Eroica*, and then decided to televise it as well. He engaged the services of a television director from Music and Arts in London, Robin Lough, who, to my delight, was someone I'd already become acquainted with through the inter-departmental concord at Kensington House. Fortunately, it wasn't live, as after a few minutes, and nicely into our stride, the floor manager stepped forward, stopping us, and apologising profusely, as there were some problems with one of the cameras. This was an unfortunate occurrence and not conducive to concentration, but thankfully the broadcasting and television experience afforded to me in London came to my aid, and with the orchestra's willingness and sympathetic understanding, the potential problem was averted, and Beethoven's magnum opus safely negotiated.

I was then invited to join the orchestra on a visit to Berlin. After the concert, we were all lavishly entertained in the British Army's headquarters in Spandau. A colonel invited Jean and myself to accompany him and his wife the next day into East Berlin. We registered our visit at the headquarters, establishing that the very latest we could cross back over the border was five o'clock that afternoon. Five minutes after that, and an alert would be triggered. No appearance by 5.30 p.m., and a full-scale search would be implemented. Armed with this cheerful news, we made our way to Checkpoint Charlie, the colonel's wife driving, and he in compulsory, full-summer uniform. At the barrier, the colonel pointed out two windows, one had a machine gun pointing at us, and there was a camera in the other, automatically taking our photographs. It has to be the most revealing, yet without doubt one of the most miserable Saturday afternoons I've ever had. The streets were dismal and empty, no sound of laughter and no children playing.

We marvelled at the enormous scale and lavish beauties of a museum, but were followed everywhere by two armed guards with their exaggerated, stamping gait. We made our way back through Checkpoint Charlie in plenty of time so as not to cause an embarrassing incident. That night, the colonel and his wife took us to Berlin's new concert hall, the Sinfonie, to hear the Berlin Philharmonic Orchestra. It was inevitable that the conductor should of all people be Herbert von Karajan. There was no doubting his brilliance, utter control, skill and masterful facility. But, oh dear. At the end of the concert he peremptorily dismissed the orchestra from the stage and returned countless times to bask alone in the adulation of his fawning admirers.

My period with the BBC Welsh as Associate Conductor was an interesting one. Most of the work was studio based, with much emphasis on contemporary Welsh music. As the BBC liked the unusual, I was able to programme for the first time for this orchestra, some of the lesser known symphonies of Shostakovitch. I had the occasional foray into the BBC series in St David's Hall, including a memorable Elgar first symphony, but since Merfyn Williams, a television producer, had succeeded Arnold Lewis as Head of Music, there was a massive concentration on television, with the likes of Mariss Janssons brought in to conduct a whole televised series of Beethoven and Tchaikovsky symphonies. Huw Tregelles Williams succeeded Merfyn Williams and, on his own admission, had to tread a careful, psychological path with John Drummond regarding the resentment shown towards Wales with its unique television output.

It's peculiar how a call directly from the manager of an orchestra triggers either little alarm bells or a frisson of excitement. In the case of Huw Tregelles Williams, it was the former. The French conductor Louis Frémaux had been engaged to conduct the BBC Welsh in the closing, Saturday night concert of the Swansea Festival, to be broadcast live, but had fallen ill. As well as the organ symphony by Saint Saens, there was a world premiere of a specially commissioned orchestral piece, the *Brangwyn Festival Overture*, by the Welsh composer, Richard Elfyn Jones. It was an awkward time for me as I had a Festival Hall concert on the Sunday with the Royal Philharmonic Orchestra featuring Holst's *Planets Suite*. Huw begged me to stand in for the indisposed Frenchman, as they were in dire trouble. The score of the new work was dispatched to me overnight, and I learnt it sitting in the back of a chauffeur-driven car to Swansea the next morning. I worked with the orchestra, then returned to London for rehearsals with the Royal Philharmonic Orchestra, which Huw had rearranged for me. After an extended Saturday morning session, I was driven to Battersea heliport, ferried by helicopter to Elstree airfield, and then flown in a chartered aeroplane to Swansea airport. I arrived at the Brangwyn Hall at seven o'clock, and began the live concert promptly at 7.30. I was subsequently told that some BBC executives were in the Royal Opera House listening nervously on transistor radios to see if I would arrive in time. It was considered by all an enormous success. It is said that God moves in mysterious ways. If that is so, then the stratagems of the BBC are a complete enigma, because, despite the fact I had successfully extricated the BBC from a very difficult situation, it signalled the end of my relationship with Radio Three. It was many many years before David Murray, now director of the newly named BBC National Orchestra of Wales, invited me to conduct the orchestra, Roger Wright having now established himself as Controller, Radio Three.

It's quite natural that, in terms of broadcasting, the BBC is quite rightly universally accepted as having had an enormous influence on people's lives, and music on radio has unquestionably brought the music of the masters into countless homes. However the last twenty years has seen the growth of a new phenomenon, Classic FM. In an ever-changing, competitive world, it has found a niche, its own way of attracting the public to the beauties, subtleties and beneficial properties of classical music. It's an excellent and welcome balance all round.

The associate conductorship of the Philharmonia Orchestra was naturally quite a different affair. Being one of the self-governing London orchestras, the unique demands made on the players meant that its work load and requirements were vastly different. The London concerts were always in the Royal Festival Hall, usually tied to provincial or south coast repeats or recordings. Usually the concerts were well planned, with the repertoire chosen by myself in conjunction with the general manager, in this case, Christopher Bishop, who had joined the orchestra from EMI Records. One morning, I had a phone call from Christopher explaining that Yevgeny Svetlanov, the Russian maestro, had been taken ill, and would I take over? Itzhak Perlman was the soloist in Elgar's violin concerto, a notoriously difficult work to accompany. For me, it was a wonderful opportunity to collaborate with one of the world's finest violinists, and also to hear at first hand his own approach to a very British work. Svetlanov had naturally chosen a major Russian work, and had programmed Shostakovitch's tenth symphony. I had already recorded a few Shostakovitch symphonies with the BBC Welsh, and had made a thorough study of the man and his music, a fascinating exploration. I felt very much at home with the musical idiom and thrived at the unexpected opportunity. At the end of the concert, William Relton, a brilliant former trumpeter, came to see me in his role as general manager of the BBC Symphony Orchestra. He congratulated me on a fine concert, said he was very impressed, and was going to write me a glowing assessment for Radio Three, and in particular its foremost orchestra. He contacted me sometime later, confirmed that I had not heard anything and was mystified as to why his report had never been followed up.

I remember one recording with the Philharmonia for several reasons. The repertoire was all British, with a London connection – the *London Overture* by John Ireland, Elgar's *Cockaigne Overture, In London Town,* and the *London Symphony* by Vaughan Williams. The CD front cover couldn't be more appropriate or evocative. It's a reproduction of a painting by one of my favourite artists, Claude Monet, entitled, 'London. Parliament with the sun breaking through the fog'. The sessions took place over two days in St Peter's Church, Mordern, South London, and brought home to me the intrinsic unpredictability of London travel. On the first morning, I left Harrow very early by car, and with a surprisingly clear run over Kew Bridge and down the South Circular arrived with nearly one and half hours to spare, as the producer, Brian Culverhouse, a recording veteran and elder statesman, was just beginning to set up his microphones and equipment. I resisted the temptation to leave later the next morning, and doing exactly the same journey at the same time, arrived with just five minutes to spare.

Another recording that gave me much pleasure and satisfaction was a CD of the music of Delius, its title, *A Song of Summer*, encapsulating the very essence of Delius's representation of quintessential Englishness. The CD front cover is again a Monet detail – 'Poplars on the Epte'.

The Philharmonia also became involved with me at this time in a major television project. Aubrey Singer, the seasoned, perceptive controller of BBC 2 television, had invited me to lunch. He had been responsible for commissioning the various contributions from Outside Broadcasts and Music and Arts that I'd been involved in, and on his retirement wanted to talk about his future plans. We met for lunch in a restaurant in High Street Kensington, and after a most agreeable discourse, he quizzed me on my thoughts and aspirations. I described how as a consequence of my lifelong fondness for choral music, I was intrigued and fascinated as to how different composers over the centuries had set exactly the same Latin words of the Mass, with such spectacular differences. I gave examples of how such colourful, vivid words as Sanctus, Gloria, Credo, Hosana, Dies Irae even, could fire the creative imagination in so many contrasting ways. Aubrey responded immediately, intimating that Michael Grade, newly appointed controller of BBC 1 television should hear what I had just told him. With that, to our disbelief, who should come past our table but Michael Grade himself. He greeted Aubrey, who introduced me, and said he should listen to some observations I'd just described. Michael asked me to phone his secretary that afternoon and make an appointment. Within days, I met Michael in his office in Television Centre. We had a lengthy, earnest conversation, he naturally searching and probing, with his intimate knowledge of every aspect of show business. The upshot was a proposition to present and conduct a series examining my thesis, but specifically dealing with the various movements of the Requiem Mass. The recording took place in St John's, Smith Square, cleared of all seating so that we could utilise the ample expanse to accommodate the sizeable orchestra and choral forces necessary to demonstrate our intriguing topic. Transmission was every night for one week, on the flagship BBC 1, ending on Easter Sunday with a repeat of Verdi's Requiem, which had originally been televised live, as part of my one hundred and fiftieth anniversary celebrations of the Huddersfield Choral Society. It was a significant and prestigious undertaking, highly acclaimed, and a vindication of Michael Grade's bold, adventurous and imaginative style. The following year I was afforded the same slot, again on BBC 1, but this time utilising the BBC Welsh Orchestra. The theme chosen was the journey in music from Palm Sunday through to Easter Sunday. The location for our pilgrimage was Tewkesbury Abbey, and although the recording was before the Easter celebrations, the fact that the Abbey was draped for authenticity in the traditional purple colours of Easter I found inspirational and devotional, adding significantly to the sincerity of our Easter message.

It was at this time that I accompanied the Philharmonia to the Newbury Spring Festival. I was conducting Bruckner's fourth symphony, the *Romantic*, and my father was very keen to see how I would tackle the musical challenges set by this formidable Austrian composer. I made my way to Newbury for the afternoon rehearsal, and saw my father waiting on the corner of the road, near St Nicolas Church, where the performance was to take place. To all intents and purposes he looked fine, but there was something that I saw in him, standing there, that sent an odd shiver through me. During the afternoon, the orchestra kept telling me how well my father looked, and he so enjoyed the convivial atmosphere and company of the players. The following week, my mother phoned me to say my father had been diagnosed with lung cancer, the ultimate result, as with Uncle John, of smoking.

It was 1988, and that summer, I had programmed Mahler's second symphony, the *Resurrection*, at the Welsh Proms, its first performance in Wales. The Halle Orchestra was engaged, and I had arranged with Clive Smart that we would open the Halle concerts season with the same work in September. My father was at the Cardiff Prom, my first attempt at this monumental work, both of us feeling at its triumphal, optimistic conclusion, a very close, personal, mutual satisfaction. In September, I was in Manchester with the Halle refreshing our memories of the Mahler, and at the same time preparing for a concert in St George's Hall, Bradford. I travelled to the outskirts of Sheffield to stay with my close friends, George and Nancy, as I knew my father was very poorly, and they were the exceptional people I could be at ease with. On the concert afternoon, I rehearsed the Elgar Cello Concerto with Steven Isserlis as soloist, and then worked on the *Planets Suite*. At the end of the rehearsal, I spent some time alone with the offstage female chorus. I had strong views as how to obtain the effect of the voices disappearing into the distance, and the banging of doors and whispered instructions and extraneous noises would hardly have been conducive to Holst's celestial vision. I carefully organised that they should walk down the stairs out into a long alleyway and keep moving until their sound literally disappeared into the night. Having finished with the ladies, accompanied by Nancy, I just walked the streets of Bradford, feeling very strange, unsettled and agitated. I eventually called into the hotel opposite the stage door for a quiet cup of tea, and fifteen minutes before the start of the concert, crossed the road to the hall for a quick change into evening dress. At the stage door, I was informed of a message to ring home urgently. My father had died as I paced the streets in such restlessness. I walked out onto the stage, and after acknowledging the audience, turned to face the orchestra. It was a pretty tough moment, and I had to really grit my teeth, as the assistant leader, my good friend Jimmy Murray looked up at me, and mouthed the word, 'sorry'.

After the concert, the hall organised a private line for me to talk to my mother. It was a very comforting chat, my mother, although going to miss him desperately, relieved that my father was no longer suffering. She even managed to see dry humour in the fact that it was her birthday, adding wryly that he never remembered it anyway. She made one request that I would promise to conduct Mahler's *Resurrection Symphony* at the Halle, two days later, as they had both rejoiced in the achievement in Cardiff, and my father would certainly have wanted me to continue. The rehearsal before the concert was carried out in utter silence, everyone having known my father for many years and very well aware of my situation. The concert itself was extraordinary, every sinew and muscle strained to the utmost, leading to a collective interpretation of unrestrained, blazing intensity. Here, as in Bradford two days earlier, was yet another example of having to carry on as normal, except this time it was close and personal.

twelve
SCANDINAVIA

FTER MY FATHER'S DEATH, my mother frequently came to stay with us in Harrow. She and Jean would spend many hours together, often shopping, either in London or in such haunts as Beaconsfield or the village of Pinner, north of Harrow. On one such visit, when I was working abroad, they called in for lunch at a quaint old pub in Pinner's High Street, the Queen's Head. It had been refurbished, was spotlessly clean, and run by a young Welsh couple, Huw and Jane. A few days later, Jean and my mother picked me up at Heathrow Airport and insisted I went with them to the Queen's Head to experience the transformation for myself. We were all delighted when, some time later, it was announced that Jane was pregnant. Unfortunately it was not a happy or a comfortable pregnancy, and after many scares, twin boys were born very prematurely, weighing just two pounds. They were desperately ill, but after the most amazing care in the maternity department of Northwick Park Hospital, the twins survived.

Their christening took place in Harrow Welsh Chapel, I having willingly accepted the invitation to become one of their godfathers. I first met my fellow godfather that very day. He was a detective in the Metropolitan Police, Steve Chapman, who was to become one of my closest friends. He had won a medal of honour at the age of nineteen for cunningly tracking down an armed robber, and he had that natural, instinctive characteristic of very good detectives, an eye and a nose for trouble. He served the force with distinction, spurning easy promotion in uniform to do what he knew he was really good at, including periods in Royal protection and the Flying Squad. Mind you, once a copper, always a copper, and there was an hilarious moment when the Prince of Wales graced the Welsh Proms on its tenth anniversary. The Prince obviously had his own protection, but Steve, having done the job himself, became my bodyguard for the night, following me wherever I went, even in the company of the Prince and his entourage.

Steve didn't profess to know anything about music, but enjoyed every moment of any concert I conducted. He had always wanted to hear the Halleluiah Chorus live, but for some reason something always happened to thwart him. The funniest however was a Good Friday afternoon performance of the *Messiah* at the Royal Albert Hall. The way it works out, musically and theologically, I tend to have a long first half, one interval and a much shorter second half. During the interval in the Royal Albert Hall, an announcement was made that although it was Good Friday, Bank Holiday or Sunday parking would not apply, and for people to be aware that their cars could be given a parking fine or even towed away. Steve went off to move his car, returning just after we'd performed the Halleluiah Chorus, missing it yet again. Years later while receiving treatment in hospital, although still far too young, he mysteriously fell into a coma, from which he never recovered. I, along with Carol, his partner had the awful, distressing task of agreeing to his life support machine being switched off. I can hear now how he would gleefully give me marks out of ten for my performance, he even gave me eleven one day, and his exhortation before every concert, 'all the best, mate'.

My involvement with Southern Television and its flagship arts programme *Music in Camera* meant I was building up a very good working relationship with the Bournemouth Symphony Orchestra. In those early days, concerts were held in the Winter Gardens, conveniently located in the centre of Bournemouth. I was very fond of the hall, which had an atmosphere very different from the usual Victorian-style buildings we tended to frequent. The acoustics were still good and I'm sure with a bit of foresight and not too much renovation, the Winter Gardens could have been restored to its former splendour, but it was not to be, and the orchestra moved to its present home in Poole. Paavo Berglund, the Finnish maestro, was the orchestra's principal conductor, and held the post with great distinction, expanding its appeal through highly acclaimed recordings for EMI. Paavo was in the audience when I conducted the Bournemouth Symphony Orchestra in a performance of Elgar's first symphony. He admitted he wasn't particularly enamoured with the work, but asked me if I would like to conduct the Helsinki Philharmonic Orchestra, of which he was music director. The orchestra had a brand new concert venue, Finlandia Hall, a superb-looking building spectacularly positioned on the edge of a lake. Unfortunately the acoustics didn't match its beauty, very dry and unhelpful, a perpetual sore point with the players and conductors.

Dealing with people with only a smattering of English, and a language that bore no relationship to anything I'd ever experienced before was quite new to me. Being a Welsh speaker, though, did help me, as I found I could pronounce Finnish quite easily, every consonant and vowel being pronounced, nothing silent. The climate, of course, was a different matter. It was bitterly cold in the winter, which was usually the time I went. Often arriving back at the hotel after a rehearsal or a walk to clear my head, I would find my face frozen stiff, hardly able to move a muscle, and the thermometer showing, at most, minus twenty. Apart from the standard symphony orchestra repertoire, I was encouraged to introduce British music, and they responded favourably to Walton's first symphony, and the *London Symphony* of Vaughan Williams. I was a little unnerved to be asked to conduct Sibelius's first symphony. Not only was Sibelius a national hero, but every Finnish musician was steeped, practically from birth, in its distinctive style, idiom and mode of expression, and certainly extremely familiar with every facet of his pioneering genius. Twice I rejected the invitation, but when they implored a third time, I capitulated. It was a most revealing experience, for they were happy to impart that intimate knowledge which was naturally almost in their blood, as well as enjoy my fresh approach when they realised and appreciated my own deep affection for Sibelius.

I have always felt a responsibility to perform compositions by composers of whatever country I spend time in. I felt particularly honoured to be entrusted with the world premiere of the sixth symphony by the contemporary Finnish composer, Einojuhani Rautavaara. There was certainly a sense of profundity in his music, with lively, flowing melodies, enhanced by glowing orchestral colours. Jean was with me in Helsinki at the time, and we were most warmly entertained one night at Rautavaara's home. We had a typical Finnish meat dish, in fact, reindeer stew, which had to be washed down with beer. This was certainly something new for Jean, but we both still talk of the cheerful, heartwarming sight of the drive leading up to the house, illuminated by brightly shining, heat radiating flares. The orchestral management had also requested at another time that I perform a work by another living Finnish composer, Erik Bergman. On this occasion, I was met at the airport by the orchestra's general manager, and told that the composer was pretty fussy and pedantic, liked to attend all rehearsals, and had invited us to dinner at his home that evening to discuss the music. He had acquired a tape recording of a previous performance, and we all sat around in his lounge listening politely. I had studied the music carefully and fastidiously and, following my score, I pointed out very tactfully that there were what appeared to be discrepancies, and wondered whether they were amendments he had made. He replied they were mistakes or an inability to produce what he had written. I assured him it was perfectly feasible to realise his intentions, as everything was well written and technically possible. Over dinner, I gently persuaded him to allow us the freedom to have the first rehearsal to ourselves, and we parted company, amicably. True to form the next morning, the players had their usual grumbles about a contemporary work, one of the reasons why I preferred the composer not to be present. Some of them even used the description, paper music. With all that out of the way, we had an excellent rehearsal, with the players admitting to a certain amount of pride and satisfaction at their ability to rattle off the difficulties.

The next morning, the composer sat in the audience seats as we confidently ran through the piece. At the end, he showed great delight, admitting he had no comments to make. Then he made one request, much to our amusement, remembering some of the earlier descriptions by the players. He asked if one of the percussionists could stand on a chair and, as a prelude to the music, slowly tear a long piece of paper from top to bottom. As a consequence of my engagements in Helsinki, I was invited to conduct other orchestras in Finland, one of them in Oulu, a good hour's flight north from Helsinki, and almost in Lapland. The hall was superb with amazing acoustics, and again I had the scope to perform unusual works such as Vaughan Williams's fifth symphony, and the seventh of Prokofiev. In the final of one of the 'Cardiff Singer of the World' competitions I had been given the responsibility of accompanying the Finnish soprano, Soile Isokoski. My appearances in Finland afforded us the opportunity to develop our musical partnership further, and she established a highly successful singing career.

My first visit to Sweden was to a town north of Stockholm, called Gävle. By this time, Arthur had had to undergo some hospital treatment, and decided to retire. I was now being looked after by Nina Kaye who, with her twin brother Tony, had formed the Kaye Artists' Management. I flew to Stockholm, and then transferred to a local flight to Gävle. Unfortunately, having flown all the way there, we had to return to Stockholm as fog had prevented us landing. After a car journey, I arrived in Gävle for a few hours' sleep before the first rehearsal. I walked from the hotel to the theatre which pleasantly, I discovered, was the home of the orchestra. On approaching the impressive frontage of the theatre I could not help notice that carved in stone were the names, Mozart and Milton, sandwiching the surname of England's greatest bard, Shakspeare, the middle 'e' omitted, unfortunately for posterity. This maiden appearance in Sweden led to visits to at least another half a dozen orchestras which, like my appearances in Finland, gave me ample opportunity to explore the often harsh, but beautiful countryside. The journey to Helsingborg, in the southwest of Sweden, could at times be quite romantic – a flight to Copenhagen, a coach to Helsingør of Hamlet fame, the castle always worth a visit, and then a ferry across a narrow strip of water. Helsingborg was where I first came into contact with Arve Tellefsen, who had played for the specially formed student orchestra at the Welsh Proms. Norway was another Scandinavian country I visited, with appearances in Oslo, Bergen, the home of Grieg, and Trondheim, with its deep fjords, where the great German battleships of the Second World War were based. Although a little later than this period, I also conducted in Reykjavik, the capital of Iceland. On one visit I woke up for no reason in the middle of the night, drawn to the window, and on pulling back the curtains, witnessed the most dazzling, dramatic display of Northern Lights. There before me was the Aurora Borealis I'd only read about in school books, tentacles, shafts and curtains of light, just mesmerising to watch.

My visits to Aarhus, Denmark's second-largest city after Copenhagen, and home to my Danish debut, were to have far-reaching consequences. The general manager of the orchestra, Steen Pade, was himself a fine musician and chairman of the Danish composers' guild. I'd met Arto Noras, the Finnish cellist, in Helsingborg, along with Arve Tellefsen when they had combined to perform Brahms's double concerto for violin, cello and orchestra. Arto had initiated, and become, artistic director of a festival in Naantali, a village on the southwest coast of Finland. He very much wished me to bring an ensemble of my choice to perform in the opening concert of the festival, and I chose the London Mozart Players. We flew to Helsinki, and were waiting at the carousel for our luggage at four on the Thursday afternoon, when an announcement came over the tannoy, would 'Mr Huge' make himself known. I was handed a message to ring London immediately. All sorts of weird calamities invade your mind, but the instruction was to ring Steen Pade in Aarhus. Apparently, the chief conductor of the orchestra was supposed to start recording four symphonies by the Danish contemporary composer, Vagn Holmboe, on the following Tuesday, but had that morning, pulled out of the project. They were in a wretched predicament, and the developments were certainly harmful for their newly established relationship with a record company. I agreed to undertake the assignment, and requested that the scores be sent directly to me in Naantali.

The first concert with the London Mozart Players was on the next day, and in the interval I was informed that the scores had arrived, and would be deposited in my hotel room. It was summertime which meant twenty-four hours of daylight, and so the whole orchestra and myself were treated to supper in an open-air restaurant at Naantali harbour. I arrived back at my hotel room at about 12.30 a.m. and there on the table was this large parcel. Curiosity, of course, has always killed the cat and so, predictably, I unravelled the parcel and started reading the scores. It was 5.30 in the morning when I noticed the time, had a few hours sleep, then met the orchestra for breakfast. I worked for the remainder of the morning, meeting the players as previously arranged to relax for a couple of hours on a boat trip. On the next day, my spare moments were spent studying Holmboe's four symphonies, while the afternoon and night were taken up with a rehearsal, and our second concert. Monday morning, I flew back to London to collect fresh clothing for the ten day period allocated for the recording. Tuesday morning was the first day of recordings, and after an early morning flight I arrived at the concert hall to be greeted, to my surprise and astonishment, in Welsh. The producer was Robert Suff, originally from Swansea, now living in Stockholm.

The record company which had instigated this enterprise was called BIS Records, based in Stockholm. Its owner was an eccentric genius, Robert von Bahr. Robert von Bahr founded BIS in 1973, aged thirty. Having studied law, statistics, music history, Finnish and Russian, he found he had to support himself in any way possible. Apart from choral singing and conducting, he followed some rather less obvious pursuits, as a professional pinball player, door-to-door book seller, taxi driver and a silver coin melter. He discovered that the silver value of certain Swedish and Swiss coins was higher than the intrinsic value of the coin. He became the Stockholm Philharmonic Orchestra's official recording engineer for some years, but with his individuality and temperament, formed his own recording company. His whole philosophy in forming his company, was to give everyone 'choice', for he felt that there are 'heaps of music out there, unknown for the vast majority of listeners, since it has never been recorded, in many cases never even performed. We specialise in sniffing out those diamonds, buried in the great rubbles of stone, in order to give the public at large the choice, the possibility to discover, to like or dislike, but to make an informed choice.' With these fundamental principles in mind, and the difficulty of convincing the general public of the qualities of contemporary music, it is rather wonderful that BIS has grown to be the world's seventh largest classical record label.

The four symphonies of Holmboe to be recorded started with number four through to the seventh. We recorded in that order, and meticulously and painstakingly completed the challenge. Robert Suff and I developed an excellent understanding, utilising every moment, but keeping a good recording pace. It was the beginning of what would become a classic producer/conductor relationship, bristling with innovative ideas, and unafraid of being progressive and adventurous. A week after the completion of the recording, Robert von Bahr telephoned to thank me for my contribution, was excited with the results, and had decided he wanted to record all Holmboe's symphonies. There were thirteen in all, and would I accept the challenge and carry through his vision? The four symphonies made a two CD set. A press launch was organised in Copenhagen, which I attended. The day was perfectly rounded off for me by the presence of Holmboe himself. He had a kind, tender nature, and set great store by the fact that he and my father were born in the same year, 1909.

In accordance with Robert von Bahr's wishes, further sessions were set up to complete Holmboe's symphonic cycle. The composer attended the first day of the next group of recordings. Danish television were in attendance, interviewing Holmboe for an arts magazine programme and it pleased us enormously that this octogenarian was being given the attention and respect he so thoroughly deserved. Robert Suff, much to my approval, contentment and ease of mind, had been made the producer for the whole assignment. His work, together with that of the sound engineer was pivotal to the success of those first CDs. During our visits to Aarhus, we had discovered the ideal bar to relax in after the effort and concentration of a punishing schedule, with a range of refreshments and excellent food. At the end of the day's recording, I asked Holmboe if he would care to join us for a beer. He replied, no, then added with a twinkle that he would come and drink red wine though. We all had a convivial evening, Holmboe happily indulging in his favoured tipple, and his wife, Meta, to our respectful admiration, drinking pints of Guinness. Naturally, I discussed with Holmboe whether he had any plans to write another symphony, and he intimated that he had some vague thoughts. We both possessed a similar sense of humour, and he chuckled knowingly when I mischievously suggested that a commission would clear the mists. Over the next year or so, the mammoth task was completed, all thirteen symphonies recorded, one of them unnumbered but bearing the title, *In Memoriam*, commissioned by the Danish Broadcasting Corporation to celebrate the tenth anniversary of Denmark's liberation from German occupation.

As it happened, a commission wasn't necessary, as on the completion of the symphonic project, Holmboe gave me the greatest possible accolade by saying he would like to write and dedicate a symphony to me, in appreciation of all our efforts. And so I gave the world premiere of his last symphony on 1 March, 1996 with the Danish Radio Symphony Orchestra in the Radio House Concert Hall in Copenhagen. Holmboe was present at the premiere, aged eighty-six, sitting alongside his compatriot and fellow composer, Hermann D. Koppel, one year his senior. This was fitting, as in the second half of the concert I was performing Koppel's oratorio, *Moses*. It was St David's Day, and I proudly wore my daffodil, together with Jean and a group of friends who had made the journey for this historic, auspicious occasion.

Over the years, our friends Calan and Malcolm McGreevy have been loyal and faithful supporters, Calan and I having first known each other as children. I of course had already been in Copenhagen for a few days rehearsing and so they were both with Jean on this trip to Copenhagen, along with my great detective friend, Steve Chapman, and his partner, Carol. The group was completed with another couple, Emrys and Jean Davies. I'd first met the two of them when I came to London as a student. Emrys sang in the Gwalia Male Choir and Jean in a ladies choir, the Dylan Singers, made up mainly of wives of the Gwalia choristers.

Emrys originated from Cardiganshire and was won of those early, brave pioneers who built up their own dairies, distributing milk to their customers in the early hours of the morning. Emrys, like a few of his friends in the Gwalia, then bought and ran a bed and breakfast hotel. Emrys is one of the funniest men I know, naturally humorous, with a never-ending stream of jokes and stories, usually beginning with the incongruous phrase, 'true story, true story'. His hotel was in Paddington, just down the road from the mainline train station, but ever one to make the most of an opportunity, the calling cards for his hotel read, Border Hotel, Suffolk Gardens, Hyde Park.

It was Emrys's birthday the day they journeyed to Denmark, and Jean asked the stewardess if he could go up to the cockpit. The request was granted, and Emrys disappeared to see the captain and co-pilot. He emerged a while later and announced to everyone, 'Ladies and Gentlemen, I'd like to inform you that today we have a lady driver, and she only looks about fifteen'. Can you imagine that happening today? Another weird thing happened on that journey. Emrys had forgotten his cufflinks and as the group walked from Copenhagen Airport arrivals terminus to catch a taxi into the city, there, on the pavement, right in front of Emrys, were a pair of gold cufflinks. He's obviously blessed with a lucky streak.

At that press launch of the initial CDs, I was approached by Knud Ketting, an authority on Holmboe, who was general manager of another Danish orchestra, the Aalborg Symphony. He was planning a special concert and wondered if I would consider conducting it. When he informed me that the repertoire included two works by Vaughan Williams, *The Lark Ascending*, and the rarely performed tuba concerto, I was sold. As a result, I was engaged for further concerts, leading to my appointment as the orchestra's principal conductor. I hadn't envisaged this possibility so, before accepting the post, I discussed it first of all with Holmboe, who was extremely keen that I should take it on, as he felt it would be advantageous for orchestral standards and most importantly for him, a boost for Danish composers. Further pressure was heaped upon me when Robert Suff and Robert von Bahr declared they would record the remainder of Holmboe's orchestral and concerto output at Aalborg if I accepted the appointment. It proved to be a fascinating period. It was certainly of enormous value for the orchestra to acquire such a recording agreement, both financially, and for its status and standing in the eyes of the musical world. The strict discipline and rigorous demands of recording doubtless led to a significant advancement in the standard of playing. The quality of the orchestra flourished as a result of this exposure, attracting fine players, and this meant extra engagements and recordings of substance for the orchestra. One such invitation was from Jesper Buhl, who owned an independent record company, Danacord, in Copenhagen. It was to record all the piano and orchestra output of Tchaikovsky, including his three concertos.

A traditional annual Christmas *Messiah* was now established and, as well as appearances in Copenhagen, Finn Schumacher, a former tuba player who had succeeded Knud Ketting as general manger, organised two tours of Germany. The first was unusual in that we were based in one place, the spa town of Bad Salzuflen, travelling to different towns and cities for our concerts. For the second tour, we travelled from North Germany staying in a different city every day, finishing in Dortmund. We had all been booked into a hotel in a park which housed the stadium of the Borussia Dortmund football team, one of the foremost teams in the Bundesliga, the German equivalent of our Premiership. Suddenly, during the afternoon, we were getting panic phone calls to return to the hotel immediately. The police warned us that as there were 80,000 fans crammed into the stadium next to our hotel, we would most likely be trapped in the hotel for hours, and probably miss the scheduled start of the concert.

And quite frankly, on returning to the hotel to collect our music and evening wear for the concert, I have never heard such a deafening, even frightening noise emanating from a stadium.

My philosophy of performing music native to the countries I worked in was given full rein during my lengthy sojourn in Denmark. On occasions, Jean was able to join me, as the children were both away at university and then in work. Apart from the vast BIS catalogue, I recorded Danish music for another company, Da Capo, either with Aalborg or the Danish Radio Symphony Orchestra, and supported the music further in live concert performances. A further by-product of my period in Denmark was to gain local insight into the music of Nielsen, Denmark's equivalent of Finland's Sibelius, a composer with whom I already had an affinity and a fondness. The relationship with BIS now developed in tandem with the expansion of their recording list into more mainstream repertoire. I had established a regular pattern of appearances with the Royal Scottish National Orchestra, due in no small measure to the fact that Christopher Bishop, on leaving the Philharmonia, had accepted the position of chief executive officer with the Glasgow orchestra. It became an agreeable balance of orchestral and choral work, as the orchestral management was responsible for a very good choir, and Christopher was keen to exploit it. The relationship continued with Christopher's successor, Simon Crookall, and together we planned, in conjunction with BIS, the complete cycle of Rachmaninov's symphonies, including the little-known *Youth Symphony*.

The London orchestra that I have probably had the longest relationship with is the Royal Philharmonic Orchestra. Two tours of the southwest of England were especially memorable, notable for the musical and social bonding that can produce extraordinary results. Early one Sunday morning, a few days after returning from one of the tours, I was phoned with the news that Sir Charles Groves had been taken ill, and would I take over that evening's performance of *The Dream of Gerontius*, at the Royal Festival Hall. Thanks to the trust and understanding built up between the orchestra and myself, potential problems which could have resulted from this were averted, with a satisfactory conclusion all round.

At a recent concert with the Royal Philharmonic Orchestra, I was reminded by one of the players of our first meeting at a festival in Estoril, Portugal, some years ago. This, in turn, triggered a memory for me. Leaving the hotel lounge to go to the concert on that occasion, I remember holding the door open for a gentleman to enter – only to discover later that the same gentleman on entering the lounge had shot someone, a bullet still embedded in the wall!

thirteen
THE NATIONAL YOUTH ORCHESTRA AND FURTHER TRAVELS

*I*T IS NOT OFTEN IT CAN BE SAID that Wales was the first in the world at something. In 1946 the National Youth Orchestra of Wales was founded by a visionary former teacher, later music inspector of schools in Wales, Irwyn Walters. The importance of youth orchestras can never be over-estimated, but Wales was the first to have a national orchestra, by name and function. It is to the everlasting credit of the founder and a succession of conductors, and the administration of the Welsh Joint Education Committee, that the orchestra has survived and flourishes today. I was well aware of the enormous contribution of the orchestra through its traditional annual appearance at the National Eisteddfod, and many excellent players in orchestras throughout the United Kingdom and beyond have come through its ranks. It was therefore quite unexpected when I was approached in 2002 to become the musical director. No Welshman had previously been assigned the post, an omission I found astonishing, as there must have been plenty of Welsh musicians before me who would have been admirable. My first, self-imposed, exercise was to appoint a new, fresh selection of tutors of the highest quality, particularly with professional orchestral expertise. Years of experience and relationships with orchestral players now came to my aid, and I personally contacted principal players from various British orchestras, a number of whom were former members of the orchestra and aware of its enormous potential. The roll call is like a list of the good and great, with principals from the London Symphony Orchestra, Royal Philharmonic Orchestra, Philharmonia, London

Philharmonic Orchestra, Royal Liverpool Philharmonic Orchestra and various BBC orchestras. It was an impeccable collection of superlative individuals, which provided me with a powerful armoury to fulfil the objectives and the aspirations already formulating in my mind.

In discussions with the players, they confirmed the psychological importance and common sense of my not being involved in the early stages of rehearsals, and the minutiae of organisation and practical arrangements. I encouraged the tutors to take full responsibility for their own sections and, just as importantly, for the individuals within. The result was that a strong trust was established between tutor and player, everyone benefiting from group as well as personal tuition. Therefore when I appeared there was a nervous anticipation, I knowing full well that the orchestra would be well prepared, and that there was quality and substance for me to work on and interpret. The choice of repertoire was crucial, and laying down a challenge vital, and so my choice of Mahler's first symphony was greeted with excitement and enthusiasm.

The training course was held at Lampeter University, an ideal campus site which, with plenty of halls of residence, could accommodate the 115-strong orchestra, tutors and pastoral staff. I was always allocated the same room on the first floor of one of the halls of residence, and it became my familiar haunt for the eight years I spent as the orchestra's musical director. The tutors would have a few days to themselves, and then my first appearance would be a rehearsal with the full orchestra. I'll never forget that first session with the orchestra, which took place in the concert hall of the Arts Centre at the university. The whole floor area, normally filled with an audience, was cleared of all the furniture and filled with the strings, woodwind, brass and harps, the timps and percussion on the stage. Right from the start, I worked with the orchestra, and treated the players exactly as I would a professional orchestra. Every person in that rehearsal room had already reached a very high standard of playing before they could even apply for an audition. That already implied a strong sense of discipline, dedication and years of practice, so the collective expertise on show augured well. I began immediately with the Mahler, the players naturally nervous at the start, but growing with confidence as I encouraged them and allowed them to play. Then, after a while, you sensed the realisation going through this body of players as they knew they were going to be part of something really special, with the potential to create a sound of power and intensity, the like of which they hadn't experienced before. It was a decisive moment from which the youngsters and I never looked back, the respect and trust mutual.

In previous years visitors had been offered the chance to sit in on an open rehearsal. Instead I suggested a concert for the locals of Lampeter as there was a large, raised area of seating in front of the orchestra. I felt it was important for the townsfolk to see exactly what had been achieved, as naturally our young people frequented the shops and cafes and had got to know the locals well. It was most encouraging that the locals turned up in large numbers, as for me this performance was very important; it gave the players, still very inexperienced, a taste of performing before an audience prior to setting off on a tour. On the course itself, rehearsals would finish at 9.30 at night, leaving time for relaxation and fun. One of the classic, annual events was the fancy dress party on a given theme, usually inspired by one of the current works being performed. The imagination on display was something to behold, with no holds barred and no outlandish trick missed to win that coveted first prize. I particularly enjoyed each year an evening of entertainment provided by the orchestra members themselves. There was really extraordinary talent on display, with jazz groups, ensembles of all descriptions, singing and dancing groups, as well as penalties set by the youngsters themselves for misdemeanours. It was all jovial good humour, part of a tradition handed down throughout the years and an essential antidote to the serious, often exhausting music-making.

Over the years our concert locations were many and varied. Cathedrals seemed to figure large, St David's, St Asaph, Hereford, Worcester and Bristol. It was important that as much of Wales as possible should be made aware of the rich talent in the youth of the country, with visits to Swansea's Brangwyn Hall, Aberystwyth Arts Centre, with its breath-taking views over Cardigan Bay, Bangor, Llandudno and, of course, the finale of each tour at Cardiff's St David's Hall. Visits were planned in different parts of England as well, for the young players to be exposed to different arduous conditions and the rigours of travel. The town hall in Birmingham had recently been refurbished, which suited us very well. Adrian Boult Hall in the Birmingham Conservatoire was also very apt and personal for me, and the long journey to the brand new Sage in Gateshead, proved to be most rewarding. From the very beginning I had expressed a strong desire that Welsh music be well represented. In the first year, because of my close involvement with Gareth Wood, I approached him to see if he had a suitable work for the orchestra. Gareth immediately offered to write a new work especially for the occasion, calling it *Above the Dingle, Stars*, adapted from a line in Dylan Thomas's poem, 'Fern Hill'. Further commissions came from Karl Jenkins, with the intriguing title, *Tangollen*, and Brian Hughes's *Troad*, based on the unexpected German bomb dropping on Rhos mountain. The Welsh composers' list was completed by Torjussen, my father, Alun Hoddinott, William Mathias and Grace Williams.

I was very fortunate to take over the orchestra at a time when its organisation was well tried and tested, guided by the practised hand and eye of the administrator, Beryl Jones, ably supported by Tony Moore. Probably the most significant appointment as I began my period was that of Andrew O'Neill as artistic organiser, Andrew being the brother of my great friend, compatriot and fellow musician, the tenor Dennis O'Neill. I had already been involved in some interesting ventures with Andrew when he was music commissioning editor for S4C, for he had a wealth of ideas and contacts, and was responsible for some enlightened and progressive arts programmes. He had a penchant for working lunches, where suggestions, schemes and thoughts would be thrashed out. One of his favourite haunts was the Ivy, a well-known restaurant in central London with a reputation for attracting the famous and notorious. One lunchtime turned out to be pretty uncomfortable for me, as a gentleman entered protected by two bodyguards, walked through the restaurant and sat down at the next table, alongside me. It was Salman Rushdie, living under the deadly fatwah issued by Ayotollah Khomeini for writing the *The Satanic Verses.*

It would have been easy and understandable if Beryl and Tony had sat on their laurels organising the youth orchestra, but together with Andrew's enthusiasm they encouraged and supported me in my determination to extend its horizons. Our first foreign trip was to Berlin, to a prestigious festival hosting the world's youth orchestras. We played in the most magnificent, traditional, rectangular hall, resplendent with chandeliers and furnishings as a result of its salvation and renovation from the former East Berlin. We knew things were going well when we received a rousing reception for a brilliant orchestral showpiece by the young Welsh composer, Torjussen. However, it was the second-half performance of Elgar's first symphony that produced an explosion of uninhibited, ecstatic applause that I only managed to stop by playing an encore. That night the whole orchestra was invited to a reception at the British Embassy, where we further entertained the distinguished gathering, sealing a triumphant visit and perhaps once again demonstrating the wealth of youth talent in Wales.

Before travelling to Berlin, and as part of our tour, we had performed Elgar's first symphony at a lunchtime concert in Hereford Cathedral. It is one of the host cathedrals of the Three Choirs Festival, and after the concert I was approached by Geraint Bowen, son of the veteran Welsh tenor

Kenneth Bowen, who was the organist and choirmaster at Hereford. He and his colleagues had been much impressed by the quality of the orchestra, and extended to me an invitation for the orchestra to appear at the next Three Choirs Festival in Hereford. The significance of this proposal was major, as this festival is the oldest in the United Kingdom, dating back to the 1700s. This was coupled with the fact that the National Youth Orchestra of Wales would be the first national youth orchestra ever to appear at the illustrious Three Choirs Festival. The concert was scheduled for eleven o'clock in the morning. By now the orchestra was becoming a formidable group, with the tutors in their element observing a palpable progress in their charges, and I, as a result of their tutelage, able to motivate and encourage the players to ever higher goals. The chosen work for that year's tour and also for this Three Choirs appearance was Mahler's fifth symphony, not only far more challenging than his first symphony but tangible proof of the enormous development since that first year. I was aware of an enormous sense of history, with works by Elgar, Vaughan Williams, Holst and scores of English composers having been premiered there, with my mentor Sir Adrian Boult gracing the rostrum on many occasions. As so often happens, the more solemn the occasion, the more surreal the circumstances in which we can find ourselves. A centuries-old cathedral naturally does not have the changing facilities required for such an orchestra, so all the girls had to dress amongst the scaffolding holding up the temporary stage whilst the boys changed in the pantechnicon used to transport the instruments. My wonderful band of youngsters were truly inspirational, and they were rewarded with the unforgettable sight of a huge cathedral packed to overflowing and on its feet, displaying genuine admiration, and soon afterwards there was an invitation for a return visit to the festival in Hereford in three years' time. Dame Janet Baker, whom I had been privileged to accompany in many exquisite moments of musical beauty and profundity, was the president of the festival, and her undisguised emotional expressions of joy and admiration will long remain in my memory.

Since the death of William Walton I'd kept in touch with his widow, Susana, and she'd frequently visited this country to attend performances of William's music, especially *Belshazzar's Feast*. She'd heard of my collaboration with the National Youth Orchestra, and invited me to bring a group of them to Ischia. Over the years she and William had created an amazing landscaped garden, full of streams, fountains, tropical plants and exotic trees and bushes, which they had collected from around the world. It's called La Mortella, the Place of Myrtles, and the villa houses a museum dedicated to the life and work of William. In 2004 it was awarded a prize as the most beautiful park in Italy. Being a small ensemble, Susana was able to accommodate everyone in the grounds of La Mortella, an amazing experience for all of us and a perfect opportunity for the players to get to know Susana more intimately. The purpose of the invitation was twofold – to perform in the Sunday concert as part of the visiting packages to La Mortella, and to participate in her experiment to create an outdoor performing venue. The main work which we presented was the original chamber orchestra version of *Façade*, the work that first made the musical world abruptly aware of Walton's originality and fertile imagination. It was most rewarding to work so closely and intensely with this ensemble, and the narrators, the singers Helen Field and Jeremy Huw Williams, responded happily and with ease.

Susana had erected a stage in the high part of the garden, with the spectacular backdrop of the village and harbour of Forio way below. Along with music by Elgar, we added extracts from William's suite *Henry V*, and his extremely taxing *Sonata for Strings*. At lunch the next day Susana and her business colleagues quizzed me about the viability of creating an outdoor performing arena. I suggested they extend the stage, as there was wasted space at the front, still retaining the spectacular backdrop but adding a sounding board to project the music, and tier the natural bowl like an amphitheatre. This work was carried out, and two years later the whole orchestra was invited to perform Walton's Symphony No. 1, for the first time on the island. That initial visit with the chamber group was naturally an emotive one for me. As a result of Walton's sudden, untimely death, his request for me to visit Ischia to study his composition had immediately become futile. This was therefore my first chance to visit Ischia, and the subsequent return to perform the symphony there was the crowning glory.

As promised, Geraint Bowen contacted me with the invitation to reappear at the Three Choirs Festival. Apparently, our performance of Mahler 5 was still being warmly and enthusiastically talked about, so there was an insistence, if at all possible, that we should perform another Mahler Symphony. Mahler 6 was suggested, but on sheer practical grounds, even simply getting the enormous orchestra onto the limited space, it was rejected. But as Hereford was really keen on a Mahler symphony, Mahler 1 was chosen. It was the centenary of my father's birth, and the orchestra's organisers felt it would be extremely fitting that we should reflect this anniversary, and so the most appropriate work was his *Prelude for Orchestra, To the Youth of Wales*. It was written and first performed in 1945 in memory of all the young people of Wales lost in the war, and it looked ahead with hope to the future of Wales that still lay in the strength of its youth. The Hereford Festival also wished to celebrate the centenary, and so it was decided that the *Prelude for Orchestra* would precede the Mahler symphony. As it happened, it was the first time any work of my father's had been performed at the Three Choirs Festival, and it proved to be a moving tribute; it was so very apt that it was being presented by the National Youth Orchestra of Wales. This performance of Mahler 1 – the response from the audience once again a standing ovation – confirmed with absolute certainty that the National Youth Orchestra of Wales was in a completely different class from that first Mahler 1, seven years earlier. It had been a mammoth undertaking at the time, a baptism of fire for all the tutors and myself, but it was an exalted, heart-warming beginning that undoubtedly laid the first foundations for the current high quality.

It was vitally important to me that the players should have a taste of all facets of professional music-making, not just rehearsals and concerts. I wanted them to experience recordings, something that was very much a part of my life and yet a very different discipline from any they had experienced. Our first CD was of Christmas music, recorded in the Brangwyn Hall in Swansea with the orchestra laid out on the floor rather than on the stage in order to utilise the space and maximise the splendid acoustics. Our second was much more adventurous, enterprising and ambitious. To celebrate the sixtieth anniversary of the National Youth Orchestra of Wales in 2006, I had invited the orchestra to perform at the Welsh Proms. As the annual course always took place in late July and early August due to school and college commitments, (the age limit of the orchestra was twenty-one) it was too late for the Welsh Proms. That particular year, a special course was planned for the Easter break, which was held in Bangor University in North Wales. Firstly, it was psychologically good for the development of the orchestra, as we had made great efforts to encourage more instrumental playing in North Wales, and attract students there to join the orchestra. The consequence was a much larger contingent of mid- and north-Walians auditioning and being accepted into the orchestra. Secondly I had organised another recording in conjunction with the Welsh Prom appearance, this time a CD of Elgar's second symphony, coupled with Alun Hoddinott's *Welsh Dances*. The Pritchard Jones Hall, part of Bangor University, has excellent acoustics, and similar to the Brangwyn we spread the orchestra out across the floor. Amazingly the CD was well reviewed, quite surprising that it should be professionally reviewed at all, and compared very favourably with its contenders.

2010 was to be my final year with the orchestra. Not only did I regard the appointment as a huge honour, but the whole period with these amazing young people was invigorating and stimulating. My own energy and enthusiasm is boundless, and together with my experience, combined with the unfettered spontaneity, eagerness and dedication of my young friends, produced a remarkable purple patch in my life.

I had been pressed very often to programme Rachmaninov's second symphony, but with harpists a-plenty in the orchestra it was important they should be well utilised. There are no harps in the Rachmaninov symphony, which meant that the harpists would have long periods not playing with the orchestra. To find a way around this problem the harps had a very busy, difficult first half, which kept them well occupied, and recitals were organised for them in all our venues, attracting a great deal of attention. We had been invited to perform at the opening concert of the St Asaph Festival which meant a great deal to me as it was originally founded by William Mathias, a composer with whom I'd had many dealings over the years, until his premature death. The festival was always in mid-September and this required splitting the normal tour. But over the years the publicity surrounding the growing success of the orchestra had contributed to growing audience numbers, with the summer tour culminating in a performance that stunned and amazed a sizeable audience in the vast arena of St David's Hall. After the summer break, the plan was to reconvene the orchestra in St Asaph Cathedral on the Friday prior to Saturday's opening night. A mark of the orchestra's growing professional attitude and aptitude was that despite the five-week gap the players quickly re-established their earlier quality, even leaving time for further fine tuning. The end result was a momentous occasion, and I wondered whether my directorship of the orchestra should have ended there, as a final concert had been arranged in the newly furbished concert hall on the Sunday afternoon at the Royal Northern College of Music in Manchester. This made sense however because its proximity to Wrexham, where the orchestra had been housed, made it easier to gather everyone together again for a further performance.

Each year, at the end of every tour, the orchestra had kindly and generously presented me with a gift. As one would expect, the youngsters were always full of imagination, coming up with an array of presents including Welsh gold cufflinks, which I wear always, a portrait, a specially designed waistcoat and bowtie to wear on the last night of the Welsh Proms, and this last year, a specially commissioned oak carving called 'Echo' by Dominic Clare. It's large and very heavy, and was wheeled into the hall at the end of the rehearsal. There was no danger of an anti-climax after St Asaph, just a beautiful way to bring down the curtain on a highly satisfying phase in my life, constant reminders of which I enjoy as youngsters whom I watched develop over the years now occupy prominent positions in major professional orchestras.

This National Youth Orchestra of Wales period coincided with a further development in my relationship with professional orchestras. I had been involved with the Royal Philharmonic Orchestra in some capacity or other for many years, and so it was most satisfying to be invited to become their Principal Associate Conductor, a newly created title that expanded the scope of our activities. I had a new responsibility for concerts in the Royal Albert Hall, and an important and vital input into promoting their new London base, Cadogan Hall, an exquisitely converted church near Sloane Square. Commercial recordings were a crucial part of an orchestra's work routine, not least for their financial gains. We embarked first of all on a recording for Warner Classics of Holst's *Planets Suite*, with the additional supplement of the newly composed *Pluto, The Renewer*, by Colin Matthews, the first budget recording of the *Planets* to include Colin Matthews's *Pluto*, an 'appendix' to the original suite, written as a tribute to Holst.

The Royal Philharmonic Orchestra decided to promote its own recordings, and my contribution to this enterprise was a disc of opera choruses, arias, duets and orchestral intermezzi. This was followed by a CD of choral classics, which encapsulated decades of my choral endeavours. There was another recording collaboration which gave me a great deal of personal pleasure. Through the support of Dame Janet Baker and the Foundation for Sport and the Arts, I obtained sponsorship for a recording of six of my father's orchestral works. Entitled, *Anatiomaros*, the name of one of the pieces, it traces my father's compositional output from the 1940s through to his last decade. These are all premiere recordings, and for someone who had so unselfishly promoted the music of others, a right and proper tribute. BIS Records was the recording company who undertook the assignment, which perfectly fitted their proclaimed ethos of spotlighting the unusual. BIS Records and I also co-operated on another venture. I had formed a chamber orchestra, Camerata Wales, in London, mainly comprising Welsh musicians of outstanding calibre. Concerts in London had attracted much interest and attention, and I was offered financial support to record with the orchestra. BIS Records decided to employ the orchestra for an interesting addition to our Holmboe series, an extended suite for strings, called *Kairos*, one of Holmboe's most difficult and demanding compositions. The next CD was a potpourri of music by Elgar, Delius, Holst and Warlock, with the addition of a premiere recording of my father's *Fantasia for Strings*. The disc has a wonderfully evocative title, *Through Gold and Silver Clouds*. It's an actual quote from Elgar, who, having flown to Paris in the early 1930s to visit Delius, described his fellow composer's music as travelling through gold and silver clouds.

Although BIS made its name and reputation with its pioneering record-ings, it also embarked on the music of more established composers. In addi-tion to our recordings of the Rachmaninov symphonies I was engaged to accompany the young Japanese pianist, Noriko Ogawa, in Rachmaninov's four piano concertos and the *Paganini Variations*. The orchestra was the Malmö Symphony in southern Sweden, a city directly across the water from Copenhagen, now joined by a beautiful bridge the construction of which I witnessed on my many visits to Denmark. BIS had also been very interested in my association with Walton and his music and a collaboration between the Walton Trust, the Orchestre Nationale de Lille in France and BIS, resulted in the first CD to incorporate both Walton symphonies. Years earlier, at our first meeting, Walton had revealed how upset he had been at the critical response to his second symphony. He could not understand why he was expected to write another symphony similar to his first, written nearly thirty years earlier, and he expressed to me his adamant belief that his second symphony was far superior. The fascinating outcome of recording both symphonies consecutively was that comparisons were immediate. The French players didn't know either symphony, so there were no preconceived conceptions or biases. Like me, the players felt that the undoubted maturity inherent in the second symphony's advanced tonality, brilliant orchestration, and tautness of construction was striking and unmistakable, certainly a real but exciting challenge to conductors and players.

As my daughter Lisa is a teacher, we try if possible to arrange holidays to coincide with her half term, either in October or February. One particular February, Lisa and her husband James went to Cape Town to visit James's younger brother William, who was staying in a vineyard nearby, completing a wine-management course. The owner was a real brute of a man, dreadful to work for, drunk most of the time and thoroughly obnoxious. They both went to South Africa to give William support, and encourage him to stick it out and complete his time there. Jean and I were unable to accompany them as I had commitments, but Lisa came back saying that we had to go to Cape Town, it was so fantastic. The following year the four of us flew out there together. Somehow the Cape Philharmonic Orchestra heard I was in Cape Town and

I was invited to meet the chief executive, Louis Heynemann, and Sergei Burdukov, the artistic director, one morning for coffee. We chatted amicably and they requested that I listen that week to the orchestra in a concert, which consisted of two piano concertos, Rachmaninov's second and third. When the pianist started on a series of encores, I quickly disappeared.

A few months later I was contacted by Sergei Burdukov, who was also the principal oboe – formally from the Bolshoi Orchestra – who issued an invitation for me to conduct in Cape Town. The orchestra was quite an interesting mixture of nationalities, mainly Eastern European, a few from the United Kingdom, and South Africans. The original Cape Town Philharmonic Orchestra had been disbanded as a result of the political turmoil, and courageously reformed when things had settled down as the Cape Philharmonic, thanks to the sterling initiatives of Louis, Sergei and their colleagues in trying and difficult circumstances. They did not have any titled conductors, but on my next visit I was offered the post of Principal Guest Conductor. Rehearsals took place in the Arts Centre which also housed the opera theatre, and concerts were held in a beautiful Victorian style City Hall, where our present Queen Elizabeth, as Princess Elizabeth, had made a speech on the balcony on her twenty-first birthday. Years later Nelson Mandela was to stand on the very same balcony, rejoicing at the end of apartheid.

I enjoyed my work in Cape Town enormously, building up a large, strong audience base which is very supportive of our efforts to develop the orchestra and raise its profile.

Sergei still has influential friends and colleagues in Russia, and he revealed to me a project that he had been working on for some time. Schnittke, the most important composer to arise in Russia since Shostakovitch, had written an oratorio, *Nagasaki*, describing the atomic bomb explosion which brought an end to the war with Japan. After a great deal of research, and clearing up anomalies in the orchestral parts and scores, I conducted the first public performance of *Nagasaki* in Cape Town City Hall on 23 November 2006, almost half a century after its creation. BIS Records had already embarked on a scheme to record a substantial amount of Schnittke's output, and were thrilled at the prospect of adding *Nagasaki* to their list. During the research into *Nagasaki* another early work of Schnittke's was discovered, the symphony 0, performed only once by students in the Moscow Conservatory as a composition exercise. After a little persuasion Schnittke's widow gave us permission to record this symphony on the same disc as *Nagasaki*. Our pioneering work for the music of Schnittke was not yet finished. He had written a ninth symphony, left-handed and with considerable effort after a series of strokes. It was virtually impossible to read, but a German scholar spent two years putting the full score together. As we had already recorded his very first symphony, BIS decided they would like us to close their Schnittke symphonic cycle with this ninth symphony, and although it's incredibly difficult and desperately awkward, the satisfactory closure was achieved. The symphony was coupled on the CD with another first, a world premiere recording of Schnittke's Concerto Grosso No. 1 for two violins, arranged by the composer for flute and oboe, the soloists being Chris Cowie, principal oboe of the Philharmonia Orchestra, and Sharon Bezaly, wife of Robert von Bahr, and described by *The Times* as 'God's gift to the flute'.

Alongside the groundbreaking performances and recordings, and the standard repertoire expected of a symphony orchestra, the Cape Philharmonic performed, for the first time, Elgar Symphony One, Mahler Symphony One and Bruckner symphonies three and four, opportune occasions for me to pursue my love of Bruckner. I certainly derived huge pleasure and satisfaction from conducting their choral concerts. The Apostolic Church was a strong, integral part of life in the suburbs and townships of Cape Town. Imagine my joy in rehearsing and performing the requiems of Mozart, Brahms and Verdi, as well as Beethoven's *Missa Solemnis* with its choir of mostly black youngsters. They would turn up for concerts in shining, spotless white shirts and blouses, totally uninhibited as they sang ecstatically, without any copies. The performance would first of all have taken place in our normal Thursday series in the City Hall, which we then repeated in a three-thousand-seater church in one of the many townships surrounding Cape Town. In the same way as when we perform in cathedrals in this country the Dean would usually give a blessing, so in Cape Town the Bishop would do likewise. Also, every rehearsal with the choir would begin and end with a prayer. An amusing incident occurred at a concert the orchestra and I gave in Kirstenbosch, the fabulous, world-famous, botanical gardens. I had to introduce the various orchestral items, and at one point explained to the audience that I didn't have a very good record or reputation for outdoor concerts, because it always rained. There was much amusement as it never rained there in the summer, and we were supposedly pretty safe. Within minutes of speaking it began to rain, clouds having been drawn down over the back of Table Mountain. The result was hysterical laughter from a seven-thousand-strong audience.

During this decade, I was also thriving on my involvement with the Royal Philharmonic Orchestra. Apart from concerts and recordings, we set off together one morning on a foreign trip that was going to test and examine our resolve and professionalism to the utmost. It was arranged that we should all meet at the Eurostar Terminal, which at the time was at Waterloo Station, where we were to catch a train to Brussels. From there it was a coach journey to perform in a festival in southern Holland. We gathered at Waterloo, had a pleasant journey, and were approaching Brussels when I heard one of the Royal Philharmonic Orchestra management sitting behind me answering a phone call loudly, with exclamations of total shock and incredulity. News was beginning to percolate through of bomb blasts on the tube network during the rush hour in London.

We arrived in Brussels with everyone now deeply concerned, as making contact to elicit any information about family and friends was getting more and more difficult. To add to our discomfort, it was pouring with rain, and the coaches to take us to Holland had gone missing. Eventually they arrived, and we set off for Holland. Half an hour later, I noticed we were back where we had started, the coach drivers having got lost. Finally we came to a motorway which seemed to lead in the right direction, but then we came to a halt, having come upon a serious road accident. We arrived at our hotel, desperately late, to be met by hoards of television and radio interviewers. Someone had tipped them off that a London orchestra was due to arrive there. The chairman of the orchestra, a very sensible viola player named Andrew Sippings, and I, suggested to the players to do what was most comfortable for them, have a meal or a sleep.

A time was arranged for us to be bussed to the concert hall for a short, late, seating rehearsal. Arriving at the hall, we were met by more media, and I did a serious interview on national Dutch television. I was continuously pressed as to why we were still in Holland and not on our way back to London. Surely, they insisted, we would prefer to be at home. I quietly and, I hope, with dignity, explained we were professionals, with a duty to fulfil our obligation. Moreover, the hall was already beginning to fill to its 5,000 capacity and it just wasn't in our nature to capitulate. The programme was Walton's *Portsmouth Point Overture*, Elgar's *Enigma Variations*, and after the interval, Tchaikovsky's fourth symphony. Luckily we had rehearsed in London the day before, so we were not going into the show totally unprepared. In the concert, after playing the overture, I turned and spoke to the audience. I explained we would play the symphony now and the *Enigma* after the interval, the Elgar performance to be dedicated to the memory of those who had lost their lives so tragically that morning. Unlike the cynicism of the media trying everything to get some sensational story, the audience really appreciated our efforts and loudly demonstrated their approval. It had been a long and difficult day, dominated by apprehension and worry, but the indefatigable spirit and determination of the Royal Philharmonic musicians shone through. My thoughts, like everyone around me, instinctively went back to 9/11. I certainly never envisaged in my musings in Glasgow airport that we would also suffer a terrorist outrage, creating our own tragic date, 7/7.

fourteen
AND FINALLY...
OR, THE LIGHTNING
CONDUCTOR

MUSIC IS MY CAREER, and by its very nature it is all embracing. The path I eventually chose demands dedication and a great deal of sacrifice, especially by the family. Jean, once I had become established, was able to give up teaching to concentrate on bringing up our children, in what was inevitably going to be a bit of a topsy-turvy world. Building up a career obviously necessitated periods away from home, leaving Jean with the everyday routine of seeing to the children's welfare and their ever-growing needs. Whenever I was home though, we were always together, an extremely close and supportive family which persists to this day, for which I will be always eternally grateful and indebted.

On completing her A Levels Lisa did not immediately wish to pursue further education in the academic sense. She spent a year studying shorthand, typing and IT skills, which would eventually serve her well, as did the ability to walk upright with a book on her head and to exit a car without displaying her underwear. Armed with this knowledge, she gained priceless experience as a PA to a project manager building a bank in the City near Liverpool Street Station, handling his business partners as well as the hundreds of mainly Irish builders. One day, she informed me she was ready to pursue the career she'd always felt was right for her, teaching, but with the added caveat that she wanted to specialise in teaching children with special needs. This instinctive care for special-needs children had manifested itself on holiday. We had discovered a quiet, unspoilt cove in the northwest of Mallorca, which we found ideal for relaxing and recharging the batteries. Often over the years, the same families would appear, the children resuming their friendships. One couple had a daughter, Maria. She was absolutely delightful, but at twenty she only had a mental age of a girl of five. Lisa handled her with firm but tender care, so that she was always part of the group.

We were advised that Oxford Polytechnic, now Oxford Brookes University, was by far the best college for this speciality, and she duly embarked on an excellent, four-year course, which quite correctly as it transpired, included a great deal of time actually in the classroom. Having graduated with a degree in education, she has steadily grown through the education system, and is now the deputy head of a large primary school in Harrow, with a specialised autistic unit serving the whole community.

Whilst a student at Oxford, Lisa had met James, who was studying land management at the same college. After working as a surveyor for a London firm, he decided to follow his father's footsteps in the banking world, rising progressively through the ranks in different banks and now working in the investment division of the American bank, J. P. Morgan, in Canary Wharf. It sounds pretty simple and straightforward, but they have both worked very hard and diligently to achieve their respective positions. After living in different parts of London, they have now settled down in, of all places, Harrow on the Hill.

Lisa had always been keen on an autumn rather than a summer wedding, and the ceremony was duly set for October, 1999. Since moving to Harrow on the Hill, we had been worshipping at a beautiful old church on the Hill, St Mary's, consecrated by St Anselm in 1094. The Vicar, the Reverend Tim Gosden, was to marry them, and knowing of the close connection with Eifion Powell, who was also Lisa's godfather, he very kindly and generously invited Eifion to share the service with him, and also give the address. Come the day itself, I think Lisa began to rue ever choosing autumn, for the weather couldn't possibly have been worse. It was absolutely atrocious, and I'd arranged for a friend to drive Lisa and me to the church in his renovated 1935 Bugati. As we arrived at the church, the rain became tropical, with Lisa and me marooned inside the car for ten minutes as the storm raged around us. Eventually, as it subsided just a little, a dozen men with large golf umbrellas formed a covered arcade for us to wade our way up the path to the church, and the precipitation had been so awful that water began running down the inside of the church walls.

However it all seemed to create a Dunkirk spirit, and the atmosphere was quite amazing. Naturally Lisa and I had to have a male voice choir, and my friends of the Cwmbach Choir did the honours. As Jean and I had unknowingly organised our wedding in the middle of the football world cup in England, so

Lisa and James's wedding day was in the middle of the rugby world cup. Wales were playing Australia that day and some of the Cwmbach had earpieces, listening to hear how Wales were progressing. Alas, we lost. However, to James's chagrin, England also lost.

After the ceremony, and a powerful rendition of Lisa's choice of Widor's Toccata to leave the church, the rain had thankfully ceased and we all walked the few hundred yards to the Master's dining room at Harrow School. From the window there is a magnificent view of the whole City, the skyscraper buildings of Canary Wharf clearly visible. However, what was really exceptional and unforgettable on this occasion was an extremely clear, bright double rainbow filling the sky between us and the City. Magical.

Geraint was educated in the John Lyon School, Harrow on the Hill, an independent boys' day school named after John Lyon the philanthropist, who originally created a school for the 'poor of the parish', now Harrow School. Geraint was at first shy at the school, but with the encouragement and clear direction of excellent teachers, he developed into a fine sportsman, captaining the school teams in soccer and cricket. He had ample opportunity to progress with his French horn-playing, and after A Level he took a degree course in Bristol, graduating in Geography. He had become very interested in sports broadcasting, and through the good auspices of Cliff Morgan, he spent a month with a BBC Radio producer for no money at all. He was the general dogsbody, but living and breathing broadcasting. He was advised to apply to as many local radio stations as possible, eventually getting a positive reply from BBC Southern Counties, based in Guildford. After reading the early morning traffic reports, he was assigned to cover Woking in the Conference League, his first break coinciding with a long FA Cup run for the non-league side. This led to a productive period as a television sports correspondent for BBC London, until he was headhunted by Sky Sports, and he is now, with an Olympics, rugby and football world cups under his belt, special correspondent for Sky Sports News.

While working for BBC London, Geraint had met Lizzie, a presenter on the children's television programme, *Newsround*. They had decided to get married in a church in the village of Cattistock, near Dorchester, in Dorset. Like Lisa, they both wanted a male voice choir, and this time I invited the London Welsh Rugby Male Choir. This was a newly formed group made up of individual singers from the London Welsh Male Choir, the Gwalia and any other choristers, as long as they were members of London Welsh Rugby Club. The choir gathered in Waterloo Station for the train journey, but as there was a strike taking place, they had to disembark at Basingstoke. They had another hour or so to wait for a connection to complete their journey to Dorchester and then on to the village, and so there were frantic phone calls to our hotel asking if we could delay the start of the wedding. They then assured us they would be on top form as they were rehearsing on the platform at Basingstoke, much to the amusement of the other stranded passengers. Where there is a church in a village, there's usually a pub, either close by or right opposite, so the wedding guests gathered in the local to await the arrival of the choir. Again a Dunkirk-like spirit enveloped everyone, although I think the word spirit this time was probably a little too literal! With the arrival of the choir, all the guests gathered in the church. The local vicar performed the wedding ceremony, and Eifion, being Geraint's godfather as well as Lisa's, gave his usual, individual-style address.

I truly rejoice in the success of my two children and, just as importantly, derive a great deal of pleasure and contentment from our close friendship. Geraint and his wife Lizzie have also given us two granddaughters, Elektra and Clementine, gorgeous nieces for Aunty Lisa and Uncle James.

Over the years we have had some wonderful family holidays, but one still stands out as very special for many reasons. We decided to spend February half-term in New York, which coincided with Presidents' Day. The day before we flew, New York had been hit by a snow storm, the remains still very visible when we arrived, in fact we nearly didn't land at all at JFK. Sunday morning dawned with a clear blue sky, but bitterly cold, the lake in Central Park frozen solid and packed with skaters. I had got it into my head that I wanted to find Dylan Thomas's pub, and after walking down the streets of Manhattan, window-gazing in preparation for a big shop, we eventually found the White Horse, with Dylan Thomas memorabilia everywhere. We had great difficulty finding this famous pub, first of all as the girls detoured into Saks, Fifth Avenue, where we boys, myself, Geraint and Lisa's husband James, enjoyed a warming cup of coffee and wondered whether – the way the girls were enjoying the shops – all our money would be gone on the first day. We were still lost when we came across native New Yorkers who, when I enquired as to where Dylan Thomas's pub was, told me to find a phone and dial 411, so that I now understood why they were always dialling this number in American films. To my great surprise I was given clear instructions as to how to find the pub, and discovered on arrival that it was next door to 10 Downing Street.

Earlier in this book, I described our family visit to Ellis Island. On returning to Battery Park we found the Marriot Hotel at the foot of the Twin Towers. As it was lunchtime we decided to eat there and discuss tactics for the afternoon ahead. We decided to go up the Towers, and asked the concierge how one goes about this. His reply was you can either go to the observation area in Tower One or there is a lovely bar and a restaurant called Windows on the World at the top of Tower Two. The views from the bar were spectacular, planes and helicopters flying way below us, and we enjoyed a few very happy hours watching the world flying by, enjoying, to our surprise, a pint of real ale from Boston – Sam Adams. As is my wont, I went on the wander, and discovered views of Manhattan in all directions. We then explored Windows on the World, and as it was Geraint's birthday in a few days we booked a table. We had the most amazing evening being thoroughly spoilt by the excellent service, hence the poignancy of 9/11.

To succeed in any profession, and mine is no different, requires purpose and single mindedness, but I do believe there is another world out there to enjoy and enhance one's life. I have been involved in many charities, beginning, I suppose, when, as a youngster in Tabernacl along with my friends, I used to stand in the streets of Cardiff with charity collecting boxes. My local charity is St Luke's Hospice in Harrow, which began as a day-care centre. I took part in many different fundraising events which culminated in the hospice becoming a full-time residential home, an inestimable boon to Harrow and its surroundings, and a much welcome relief for the overstretched local hospital. For one of the fundraising events, I procured the services of the Cwmbach Male Choir, who travelled up from Wales, free of charge. St Mary's was the setting for a wonderful evening of popular favourites, the audience revelling in the unique sound. Another of the fundraising events was put on in conjunction with Harrow School. An open-air concert was planned on the school's rugby pitch and I organised the services of the BBC Concert Orchestra, the Band of the Royal Air Force, and singers Susan Bullock and Arthur Davies. Arthur was easing into retirement, and came up for the day from the pub he owned in Ystradgynlais, in the Swansea valley. I am very glad we had the sense to hire a well-protected, dome-like stage, for of course it was absolutely lashing with rain. Even in such atrocious conditions, the support was phenomenal, and when the rain ceased and the moon came out, the atmosphere was magical.

The evening had an added poignancy. My mother had spent a most pleasurable fortnight staying with us, being quite rightly pampered and indulged, and holding court to our friends in the time-honoured way of octogenarians. On returning to Cardiff, she had fallen and broken her pelvis, and with the advent of complications, she was not expected to survive. Throughout the concert, Susan, Arthur or the orchestral manager was on the phone, and ultimately, at two in the morning, back at home, I received the sad news that she had died.

Whilst Geraint was in the John Lyon School, I was asked to become a parent governor, continuing on as a governor after he left school, not least out of gratitude for my son's education. When the chairman retired, I agreed to take on the job, inspired by the will on all sides to improve and enhance the facilities and reputation of the school, and encouraged by the redoubtable Sir Thomas Beecham's words, 'if you want anything done, find someone who's busy'. I had an excellent group of governors whom I knew well, and who between them covered most gubernatorial problems. To complete the balance of expertise I brought a financial and business expert onto the board, Paul Harrison, who was enjoying early retirement from an extraordinarily taxing job as one of the heads of Barclays Investment Group. He was a former Wasps rugby player, huge, six foot seven and almost as wide. He, when necessary, frightened the living daylights out of anyone, but he was actually soft as putty, one of my greatest friends and supporters in my fascinating work at the school. I chaired a governors' meeting once a term, and the first thing I did was to arrange a meeting with the bursar of Harrow School, an ex-army lieutenant colonel, Nick Shryane, on the morning of a meeting. We would carefully go through the agenda, outlining which decisions had to be made, and highlighting any potential pitfalls. This I found invaluable, and continued the practice throughout my six year tenure as chairman.

The chairmanship meant I became a governor of Harrow School as well, quite a revealing experience, seeing at first hand the complications, complexities and ever-present hazards of a 700 boy, world-famous, boarding school. It was yet another learning curve, and one I cherish. Harrow School has a very special employee at the school known as 'Coustos', custodian, dating back to the 1700s. During my period a Welshman was appointed, the first in the history of the school. Kevin Sincock hailed from Bryncethin near Bridgend and was taught by my rugby friend, John Lloyd. He for ever thanks John's strict discipline for preparing him for his chosen career in the Welsh Guards, becoming a reluctant and shy hero of the Falklands War. He is an invaluable asset to the school, his military mien and discipline a credit to his former regiment and an unmissable example to the boys.

Over the years, I have been the fortunate beneficiary of various accolades and presentations. However, one of the most moving gifts occurred one New Year's Eve, the day my CBE was publically announced. Kevin had a small, intimate party at his house, and at midnight he called for attention. He presented me with the silver leek worn by only the Welsh Guards, which he had worn in his beret in the Falklands War. What a humbling experience, and that leek is now worn on my lapel at every concert I conduct.

I had an intriguing request out of the blue one day, to meet a man called Johnny Moss, again an ex-Welsh Guard. I was to meet him at the headquarters of J. P. Morgan, the investment bank, where he was in charge of public relationss and sponsorship. He had been asked by the Mayor of London to organise an event to support his chosen charity, St Paul's Cathedral. The organist of St Paul's had recommended that Johnny should talk to me, hence the lunch engagement. After toying with lots of different ideas, Johnny narrowed ideas down to my suggestion of a performance of Verdi's Requiem in St Paul's Cathedral. By the time I arrived home, there was a message confirming that they wished to go ahead with this performance. As a result of Johnny's brilliant organisational skills it turned out to be quite an occasion, with the vast expanses of the cathedral echoing to the combined forces of the Royal Philharmonic Orchestra, the Royal Choral Society and the Brighton Festival Chorus, all recorded for posterity by EMI. A final, lovely touch was added as, being St David's Day, the cathedral was bedecked with hundreds and hundreds of daffodils, and the Prince of Wales with his love of music – in particular Verdi's Requiem – added his own characteristic presence and dignity.

Johnny Moss wasn't finished there. Two more concerts were organised, both of them this time at the Royal Albert Hall. The first was a mixture of classical favourites, again graced by the presence of the Prince of Wales. Julian Lloyd Webber played Elgar's emotive cello concerto, with *Carmina Burana* bringing the evening to a rousing climax. The Prince of Wales again gave his considerable support, ensuring a substantial financial contribution to the magnificent efforts of the Macmillan cancer nurses. The second was a gigantic affair, nothing less than Mahler's Symphony of a Thousand. The Royal Philharmonic Orchestra and the Royal Choral and Brighton Festival Chorus were augmented by the Philharmonia Chorus and London Philharmonic Choir, the four of them creating a perfect balance for the two separate choral groups needed to realise Mahler's colossal vision. The beneficiary this time was the Royal Albert Hall itself, its completed restoration and that of the organ hugely appreciated and enjoyed by both performers and audiences alike.

Mahler's Symphony of a Thousand featured once again in another charity event in which I was involved. Michael Grade had left the BBC and was now chief executive of Channel 4. After the successes of our earlier ventures, he was keen to involve me in another major enterprise, so we decided to support the Prince of Wales who had just launched his Salisbury Cathedral Spire Appeal. The Mahler symphony was to be the work, and Dave Heather of *Music in Camera* and Southern Television fame, would direct a live transmission for Channel 4. The Prince of Wales agreed to record an introduction to the broadcast, which Dave Heather and I duly planned in Highgrove, the Prince completing his talk to camera in one impressive take. The cathedral of course lent itself to this event admirably, with its spatial and visual properties, the huge, raised forces creating a spectacular vista both in the cathedral and on television. In order to achieve the utmost separation, I was able to place the soprano, Amanda Roocroft, in the part of Mater Gloriosa, way up high, virtually in the cathedral's ceiling. It was also very fortunate that we had decided to pre-record the Prince's message, rather than do it live, as a few days before the transmission he was unseated from his horse during a polo match and broke his collarbone.

The Prince of Wales over many years has been a great friend of the arts and I have benefited personally from his support. Came his sixtieth birthday and I was able to return the favour. At midday on the actual day of his birthday, I presented and conducted a concert in the Floral Hall of the Royal Opera House which featured the Philharmonia Orchestra, six children's choirs representing Wales and different English regions and, would you believe, sixty harps. It was a remarkable occasion and a children's choir of 200 singing 'Happy Birthday' was clearly appreciated by the Prince, and his response to the media was, 'It has been the best birthday I could have possibly imagined and thank you all so much.'

One particular charity request turned out to have rather unforeseen consequences. Meirion Thomas, my student medical friend, now a cancer surgeon, and Bob Phillips, the oncologist, asked me if I could raise money for some essential, specialised equipment for the cancer unit at Westminster Hospital. The outcome was a concert at the Royal Festival Hall, with John Lill also donating his services, the orchestra being the London Philharmonic. Princess Diana added her own unique lustre and charm and a large sum was collected to provide the much-needed equipment. Some years later, after Jean's cancer operation she was sitting in the reception area of Westminster Hospital waiting for Bob Phillips to arrange her radiotherapy treatment, when she noticed on the wall a plaque commemorating the charity concert at the Royal Festival Hall, conducted by myself. It later transpired that Jean was treated with the very equipment that the concert proceeds had procured.

I was very fortunate to have enjoyed the company of a number of Welsh Lords and shared their many and varied reminiscences. Lord Elwyn-Jones held the high office of Lord Chancellor, Baron Cledwyn of Penrhos was a former Secretary of State for Wales and Leader of the Opposition in the House of Lords, and Lord Edmund-Davies was the judge who presided over the trial of the Great Train Robbers. It was through them that I first became acquainted with George Thomas, the redoubtable Speaker of the House of Commons, later Viscount Tonypandy, famous the world over for his inimitable incantation, 'Order, Order'. I had become, first of all, a vice president of the National Children's Home, later renamed Action for Children, and then a founder patron of the George Thomas Society, formed to deal with special needs within Action for Children. In order to aid Viscount Tonypandy in his patronage of the charity, I conducted a performance of the *Messiah* in Westminster Abbey, a gentle, tranquil evening, very different from the large, rousing canvases of Mahler, but just as inspiring and worthwhile for the charity nonetheless.

Two incredible events of a vastly different nature from anything I had previously been involved in gave me as much pleasure from their sheer scale and audacity as from the gain to the charities. David Wyndham Lewis, a man of extraordinary entrepreneurial skills, collected together in the Cardiff Arms Park a male choir of 5,000. Instead of an orchestra, he obtained the services of the Bands of the Household Division, who had only been conducted once before by a non-military person, and that was Sir Adrian Boult. The day itself was very hot, eighty-five degrees by the afternoon rehearsal. As I was conducting, a seabird dived low in front of me and then swooped up sharply again, triggering a childhood memory of impending storms, which I quickly banished to the back of my mind, comforted by the scorching heat and cloudless blue sky. A few hours later, resting in the hotel, I heard the first rumble of thunder. Apparently, thunder storms move up the Bristol Channel, but if they turn inland, Cardiff, because of its geographical position, gets a real pounding, which is exactly what happened on this occasion. The choir and audience were comfortably dry in the stadium stands, but the stage, holding myself and the band, was out in the open, totally exposed to the elements. The bands were well-kitted out and used to performing outdoors in inclement weather, which would have been impossible for a symphony orchestra with the wrong clothing and highly expensive, sensitive string instruments. I was wearing a black mackintosh over my tails, which the music director of the band advised me to keep on, to take the sting out of the battering I was about to take. A walkway had been built up the middle of the stage for entrances and exits, and as I looked up to start my ascent, I was met with a river of water cascading towards me, and a deluge of rain smacking into my face. Needless to say, there was nothing else for it but to battle on, and as the live television pictures showed, the conditions provided a concert of extraordinary drama and quality. No wonder I was gaining a dubious reputation for outdoor concerts! By the time our star guest, Tom Jones, appeared, the storm had subsided, and we were back to a semblance of normality. Tom Jones I found absolutely charming and a joy to work with, and at the end of the show when I had been peeled out of my soaking-wet clothes, he and I had a quiet beer together. David Wyndham Lewis and I were both Lords Taverners and so all the proceeds went to buy Sunshine coaches for that amazing charity. The guest of honour that night was the President of the Lords Taverners, the comedian Leslie Crowther who, in his own incomparable fashion, having seen the thunder storm raging around me, christened me 'The Lightning Conductor'.

Two years later, David went even further, creating a male choir of ten thousand, the choristers travelling from all parts of the United Kingdom, and as far afield as South Africa. This time we were accompanied by the Royal Philharmonic Orchestra, but made sure everyone was well sheltered from the weather. Shirley Bassey was our star guest, and I had a rehearsal with the orchestra in London prior to the event to check all the music, especially Bassey's numbers. She was already well known for being a little difficult on occasions, and apparently her journey down to Cardiff had been rather fraught. On arrival, her opening number was changed, her musical director handing out the music to us. We sight-read the new piece perfectly, and with no problem, to his, and Bassey's amazement. We had an encore up our sleeves, and after completing Shirley's routine, I launched into 'Hey Jude', ten thousand men singing the chorus like she had never heard it before. At the end of the rehearsal, Shirley's music director came up to me and said I'd got away with it that time, but that she'd never do the encore on the show. I'm up for a challenge any time, and in the concert, at the end of her programme, I bent down from the rostrum, whispered in her ear that Tom Jones had sung an encore the previous year, to which she had no answer. The encore naturally brought the house down. Most importantly, Macmillan Cancer benefited enormously from a spectacularly successful evening.

Diana, the Princess of Wales, in her tragically short life, contributed enormously in her tireless, unselfish manner, to many charitable causes. A concert was arranged at Cardiff's International Arena to provide funds to establish the first children's hospice in Wales. Princess Diana immediately endorsed this essential and badly needed service, and underlined her support by attending the concert. Luciano Pavarotti was engaged as the star attraction, but the Royal Philharmonic players had warned me of Pavarotti's extreme and excessive demands, and with great hilarity and humour described some of the dubious antics they had suffered. On this particular occasion, Pavarotti insisted on a very expensive private jet to fly him to Cardiff, and despite having four British opera singers in the line-up, insisted on an American soprano being flown by Concord from New York to sing one duet with him. To add to the already colossal expenses, he further insisted on a sizeable retinue of managers and attendants, and his own conductor, just to conduct his two arias and a duet. The organisers were aghast at this latest imposition, but I can honestly say it didn't really bother me as I had plenty to do conducting and organising a lengthy concert, and most importantly ensuring an unqualified artistic and monetary success.

During Pavarotti's contribution, I went back to my dressing room to quietly gather my thoughts. The intention was to create a tableau of all the artists who had taken part in the space in front of the orchestra. I would make a speech describing the pioneering children's hospice movement, and we would round off the occasion with the Welsh National Anthem. Unfortunately, Pavarotti had different ideas, and caused chaos by trying to include the onstage choirs in an unplanned encore, 'Libiamo', from Verdi's opera, *La Traviata*. No one knew the Italian words or the music, and the whole thing dissolved into total disarray. Meanwhile, our two presenters from Harlech Television had been told by one of Pavarotti's minders in rather obscure, colourful language, unprintable here, to get out of the way, as Pavarotti was now in charge. Emerging from my dressing room and surveying the shambles, the broadcaster in me took over. Pavarotti always demanded a ramp had to be built up the middle of the stage, bisecting the orchestra and ensuring a dramatic entrance for him. I walked up the ramp, whispered to the two presenters who were standing helpless by their microphones to cue the last item, which I then performed with the orchestra and choirs. Our beautifully arranged tableau was now in ruins, and the four singers and a couple of ballet dancers shuffled onto the stage alongside me. I had to descend from the podium to make my speech, but the singers were blocking my path to the microphone. As I stepped down, one of the singers stepped backwards, pushing my leg away. Normally, this would not have been a problem, but Pavarotti had hidden a loud speaker behind the microphone so he could have a feed of the orchestra's sound, despite the fact he was already standing in the middle of the orchestra. As I stepped down, my foot twisted badly on the angled loud speaker. Standing at the microphone, I knew I had done some serious damage but completed the speech, clambered back on the podium, and led performers and audience in the national anthem. It transpired I had badly torn ligaments and spent the next seven weeks on crutches.

The next morning, Jean and I flew to Mallorca for a week's break in Puerto Pollensa, in the beautiful northwest of the island. I was in agony, and although well looked after in Heathrow, things were not so good over the water. Having been taken in a wheelchair from the plane on landing, I was dumped by the baggage carousel, and left to my own devices. I had rented a car, but even the rental company took pity on me, and cancelled the booking, realising it would be impossible for me to drive. Jean certainly wouldn't drive on the wrong side of the road! The next day we went by taxi to the little Cala which we usually visited in the summer to see the doctor, who contacted the pharmacy in Puerto Pollenca and arranged for me to buy a pair of crutches the next day.

This is where sometimes, in the most painful of circumstances, there is a silver lining. My knight in shining armour turned out to be a taxi driver, Lorenzo. He had picked us up at the hotel for the journey to the pharmacy, and was so concerned, he waited until I had my crutches and looked after me until he felt I was properly organised. He is now a firm friend on the island, my family and friends' personal taxi driver.

People have always fascinated me, and my profession has afforded me the chance to travel to places I would not normally have expected to visit, and to come face to face with an assortment of characters and personalities. They include prime ministers, presidents, chief constables as a result of dealing with royalty, church leaders and, of course, sports people. As a result of John Lloyd's long and distinguished career in Welsh rugby, I enjoyed the company of many Welsh rugby internationals. Gerald Davies I first met on a trip to Edinburgh, in the North British Hotel, the focal point for all players and spectators at Scotland/Wales confrontations. It heralded the beginnings of a life time of friendship, a barmy mixture of rugby and musical anecdotes, and serious observations on life's capriciousness. Gerald is a highly intelligent man and a writer of class and substance.

Barry John has always been one of life's delightful characters whom I meet either in Cardiff or on his visits to support London Welsh rugby. John Dawes, Barry's Welsh and British Lions captain, takes his role as president of London Welsh seriously, a regular visitor to Old Deer Park, joining his fellow 1971 London Welsh Lions team mates, Geoff Evans, Mike Roberts and John Taylor in convivial, after-match banter. Particularly agreeable were my discussions with Carwyn James, that wise tactician, who coached the victorious Lions so brilliantly. It will always remain a mystery to me why the Welsh Rugby Union never appointed Carwyn as Welsh coach, refusing to acquiesce to his sensible wishes to be solely in charge of the direction and destiny of the team, rather than it being run by a committee. The jocular nature of the players was probably best summed up when my son Geraint, then a little boy, asked Gareth Edwards, one of the world's great scrum halves, for his autograph. He wrote, 'don't be a donkey number 3 like your uncle John (John Lloyd) be a star number 9 like me".

Jean and Neil Kinnock first met when they were among a choir of forty chosen to sing in the Arms Park (which has today, of course, made way for the Millennium Stadium) for the opening ceremony of the Empire Games in Cardiff, in 1958. Glamorgan Education Authority had some progressive thinkers at the time, wishing to develop the concept of that original event. Choral and orchestral courses were organised at Ogmore by Sea, leading to a dramatic increase in instrumental teaching and eventually resulting in scores of players succeeding in the music profession at the highest level. Neil, like Jean and I, met his future wife Glenys, who was from Holyhead in Anglesey, at Cardiff University. Although I got to know Neil as a chorister in various choirs at university, I was well aware of his burgeoning political aspirations as he became a strong, purposeful president of the college union, his ambitions fuelled by his hero, Aneurin Bevan. As families in London, we enjoyed a healthy friendship, never allowing work or politics to interfere. When he became leader of the Labour Party, I sent him a handwritten letter congratulating him, but also advising him there would be some extremely tough, arduous times ahead and that our home would always be a haven. It proved to be very much the case one Saturday. We had arranged for the Kinnocks to join us at our house to watch the Ireland/Wales rugby match on television. Stephen, their son, now married to Denmark's Prime Minister, arrived in plenty of time to settle in and be comfortable for the afternoon's viewing. Neil and Glenys arrived late, looking exhausted, ashen and shell-shocked. Their long-standing, loyal agent had died suddenly the day before in his constituency in Wales, devastating them both and exposing them mercilessly to media scrutiny. In the total privacy of our home, they relaxed and returned to some semblance of normality.

Whatever one's political affiliations, Neil is well respected. He's a good, honest man. He has always called me the sensitive one, because he admitted he had to have a thick skin to survive in politics. Imagine my surprise when one day I had a phone call saying that he and Glenys had been deeply upset by an incident, and would I meet up with them. They described how they had been a guest in the BBC box at a Promenade concert in the Royal Albert Hall. Glenys in her inimitable way, had mentioned my name. John Drummond, still Controller of Radio Three and director of the Proms, retorted, 'that rugby-playing, Welsh band master, will never appear in my Proms'. I have yet to be invited to conduct at the London Proms.

It's not often conductors have the opportunity to meet. Naturally, Haitink and Kempe had an important influence on me, as I was fortunately exposed to their greatness in my formative years. Giulini, on the few times I met him, had an aura of humility about him, self-effacing and unassuming. Sir Adrian Boult had that same quality, but with a stately English reserve. His concern was to be true to the composer's wishes, and the needs of the players as well as others. On arriving at the Royal Festival Hall for one of our shared concerts, he noticed Jean was heavily pregnant and offered her his chair. Despite being an octogenarian he said to Jean, 'my dear, your need is far greater than mine'. I've often wondered what it would have been like to have met Sir Thomas Beecham, apparently the complete opposite of Sir Adrian with his wicked wit and natural-born arrogance. Stories about him abound, I'm sure many of them apocryphal and not to be taken too seriously. He was said to have been rehearsing the Halle in the Free Trade Hall on a particularly drab, cold, miserable, wet morning in Manchester. The playing was rather bad, and Beecham let it continue for a surprisingly long time, and then, without stopping the orchestra, proclaimed with devastating sarcasm, 'sounds like an Eisteddfod'. I do though, have a favourite Beecham story. He was shopping, or was it browsing, in Fortnum and Mason, Piccadilly, one day, when he was approached by a well-dressed, elegant lady. She enquired how Sir Thomas was, and he had that awful feeling we've all suffered, I know this lady but who on earth is she. He began fishing around asking questions to ascertain some sort of a clue. Then he remembered that there was a brother involved somewhere. 'How is your brother?' enquired Sir Thomas. 'Very well,' was the reply. 'Is he in good health?' persisted Sir Thomas. 'Absolutely.' Sir Thomas blundered on, 'and what is he doing these days?' Back came the withering reply, 'Oh, he's still the King.'

Although I've spent my professional life in the classical music business, I've been privileged to enjoy the company, and share the trials and tribulations of those in different branches of the entertainment industry. One person, for me, shone above everyone – Harry Secombe. I first met Harry as a result of a phone call from James Gilbert, who had produced and directed my first foray into television, the play, *Choir Practice*. He had directed a feature film starring Harry, and they had encountered a few problems, and could I meet them at Elstree Film Studios. We met up, along with Harry and his manager, James Grafton. The film began with Harry, in his native Swansea, standing in the pouring rain, enviously studying in a shop window, brochures advertising life in sun-kissed Australia. His journey to Australia began in a jumbo jet, followed by a shuttle in a smaller plane, ending with him landing on a dusty airstrip in the middle of the bush, in a single engine, tiny crate. To escape the miserable weather in South Wales, he had taken on the responsibility of a one-class, one-teacher school in the Australian outback. The kids naturally played mayhem with this Pom until Harry hit on the idea of getting them to sing. He trained them into a decent group, finally travelling to Sydney to compete in a national singing festival. Unfortunately the performances recorded in Australia were not very good and I was asked whether I could do something about it. I replied I could re-record all the music in London and post synchronise it to the existing pictures. James Gilbert now decided that the film needed some further sequences for its early stages, so we spent a week filming in Aberfan, the village that had suffered such a devastating disaster. There's a lot of time hanging around during filming, so Harry and I spent many hours together. I had always thought he had a great voice, but how could people take that aspect of his talent seriously, and how could he sing well and properly in the middle of a half hour slapstick comedy show on television?

Together, we planned a six-programme radio series, which encompassed the tenor repertoire with different guest artists to add colour and variety. We put the idea to my erstwhile Radio Two producer, Barry Knight, and the series was commissioned. Recording took place before an invited audience in the Hippodrome, Golders Green, which had become the home of the BBC Concert Orchestra. The schedule usually meant a piano rehearsal with Harry and any guest artist in the morning, lunch in a restaurant in Golders Green, a full rehearsal in the afternoon, followed by the evening recording session. One such lunchtime stands out above all others. The guest was Dudley Moore who played, among other items, a movement from a Mozart piano concerto. I left the restaurant that lunchtime with my face muscles aching from the laughter created by these two genuinely funny men, Harry having the incredible ability to make a large dinner plate stick firmly to his forehead. Genuine is a word I choose deliberately and carefully. Harry was without question a genuinely good man. Married to Myra, a Swansea girl, his family was very important to him, as mine is paramount to me. On one of our summer breaks in Mallorca, we visited Harry who had a villa on the east coast of the island. Our two families mixed easily, Lisa of course in her element, organising the grandchildren. My abiding memory of Harry will be of him standing in the middle of the road waving us goodbye and sending us on our way with a perfect top C.

I began my reminiscences with a prologue, the temptation being to close with an epilogue, but there is something too final about that. I am blessed with a wife, a warm, delightful family of two successful children, both happily married, and two granddaughters. Having chosen my path, I embarked upon a conducting career with innocence and bright-eyed optimism. That enthusiasm has never dimmed. Neither has my Christian belief, the strength of which led me to make that monumental choice between the ministry and music, guided as I have been to conduct my vocation in a way akin to the pastoral side of the ministry. With hindsight, it has dawned upon me that I probably never had a choice in the first place, the whole process being irrevocably part of my ultimate destiny.

SELECT DISCOGRAPHY

BIS RECORDS

Vagn Holmboe

BIS-CD-843/46   The Complete Symphonies and *In Memoriam*
Aalborg Symphony Orchestra

BIS-CD-802   Concertos for Trumpet, Trombone and Tuba
Håkan Hardenberger (trumpet), Christian Lindberg (Trombone), Jens
Bjørn-Larsen (tuba)
Aalborg Symphony Orchestra

BIS-CD-852   Four Symphonic Metamorphoses
Aalborg Symphony Orchestra

**BIS-CD-91   Concerto for Recorder, Concertos for Flute No. 1
and 2**
Dan Laurin (recorder), Manuela Wiesler (flute)
Aalborg Symphony Orchestra

**BIS-CD-1176   Concertos for Oboe, Clarinet and Piano; Beatus
Parvo for Choir and Orchestra**
Gordon Hunt (oboe), Martin Fröst (clarinet), Noriko Ogawa (piano)
Danish National Opera Choir, Aalborg Symphony Orchestra

BIS-CD-917 Concertos for Orchestra No. 8 and No.10; Concerto giocondo e severo; Ballet Suite: *The Ill-Tempered Turk*
Aalborg Symphony Orchestra

BIS-CD-1596 String Sinfonias I–IV 'Kairos'
Camerata Wales

Christian Horneman

BIS-CD-749 Theatre Music (music from: *Aladdin*, *Esther*, *Kalanus*, *Gurre* and *The Struggle with the Muses*)
Aalborg Symphony Orchestra

Sergei Rachmaninov

BIS-CD-900 Piano Concertos No. 2 and No. 3
Noriko Ogawa (piano)
Malmö Symphony Orchestra

BIS-CD-975 Piano Concertos No. 1 and No. 4; 'Paganini Rhapsody'
Noriko Ogawa (piano)
Malmö Symphony Orchestra

BIS-CD-1665/66 The Three Symphonies, '*Youth Symphony*',
Overture: *Prince Rostislav*, *Vocalise*
Royal Scottish National Orchestra

William Walton

BIS-SACD-1646 The Two Symphonies
Orchestre National de Lille

Arwel Hughes

BIS-CD-1674 *Anatiomaros, Prelude for Orchestra, Owain Glyndwr*,
Overture to the opera *Love is the Doctor*, **Prelude to the opera** *Menna*,
Suite for Orchestra
Royal Philharmonic Orchestra

Collection: **'Through Gold and Silver Clouds'**
BIS-CD-1589 **Elgar:** *Serenade for Strings, Elegy for Strings*; **Arwel Hughes:** *Fantasia in A minor for string orchestra*; **Peter Warlock:** *Capriol Suite*; **Frederick Delius:** *On hearing the first Cuckoo in Spring, Summer Night on the River*; **Gustav Holst:** *St Paul's Suite*
Camerata Wales

Alfred Schnittke

BIS-CD-1647 **Symphony No. 0 and *Nagasaki*: Oratorio for mezzo soprano, mixed choir and orchestra (world premiere recordings)**
Hanneli Rupert (mezzo-soprano), Cape Town Opera Voice of the Nation Choir, Cape Philharmonic Orchestra

BIS-CD-1727 **Symphony No. 9 and Concerto *Grosso* No. 1 (world premiere recording of version for flute, oboe, prepared piano and string orchestra)**
Sharon Bezaly (flute), Christopher Cowie (oboe)
Cape Philharmonic Orchestra

EMI

Verdi Requiem
Royal Philharmonic Orchestra, Royal Choral Society, Brighton Festival Chorus
Recorded in St Paul's Cathedral

Hymns Album
Huddersfield Choral Society. Gold Disc

Carols Album
Huddersfield Choral Society. Gold Disc

5000 Voices at the Arms Park
Bands of the Household Division. Tom Jones

10000 Voices at the Arms Park
Royal Philharmonic Orchestra. Shirley Bassey

Music of Paul Patterson
London Philharmonic Orchestra

ASV

Vaughan Williams – *A London Symphony*
Philharmonia Orchestra

A Song of Summer – **Music of Delius**
Philharmonia Orchestra

QUARTZ

Brahms four Symphonies
Stuttgart Philharmonic Orchestra

BBC ENTERPRISES

Sibelius Symphony 1
BBC Concert Orchestra

PHILIPS

African Sanctus, **David Fanshawe**
Ambrosian Singers

DANACORD

Tchaikovsky, Piano Concertos 1–3
Aalborg Symphony Orchestra

WARNER

Holst, *Planets Suite*
Royal Philharmonic Orchestra

INDEX